DATE DUE

AMERICAN-RUSSIAN ECONOMIC RELATIONS

1770s—1990s

Guides to Historical Issues

Richard Dean Burns, Editor

#1 WHO FIRST DISCOVERED AMERICA: A Critique of Writing on Pre-Columbian Voyages
Eugene R. Fingerhut

#2 THE MISSILE CRISIS OF OCTOBER 1962: A Review of Issues and References
Lester Brune

#3 AMERICA SEES RED: Anti-Communism in America, 1870s to 1980s: A Guide to Issues and References
Peter H. Buckingham

AMERICAN-RUSSIAN ECONOMIC RELATIONS

A Survey of Issues and References

James K. Libbey

REGINA BOOKS

CLAREMONT, CALIFORNIA

Library of Congress Cataloging in Publication Data

Libbey, James K.
    American-Russian economic relations, 1770s-1990s : a survey of issues and references / James K. Libbey.
    202 p. cm. --(Guides to historical issues : #4)
    Bibliography : p.
    Includes Index
    ISBN 0-941690-35-0
    ISBN 0-941690-36-9 (pbk.)
    1. United States--Foreign economic relations--Soviet Union. 2. Soviet Union--Foreign economic relations--United States 3. United States--Foreign economic relations--Soviet Union--Sources. 4. Soviet Union--Foreign economic relations--United States--Sources. I. Title. II. Series
HF1456.5.S624L53 1989   337.73047--dc20
                                              89-32604
                                                    CIP

Regina Books
P.O. Box 280
Claremont, Ca. 91711

Manufactured in the United States of America.

ACKNOWLEDGMENTS

One of the few pleasures I have in preparing a book for publication is acknowledging the help of those scholars who uphold the professional tradition of rendering assistance to a colleague. While I must assume final responsibility for the published work, I am particularly grateful to those who critically read portions of the manuscript: Edward M. Bennett, Professor of History, Washington State University; Josef C. Brada, Professor of Economics, Arizona State University; Lloyd C. Gardner, Professor of History, Rutgers University; Raymond L. Garthoff, Senior Fellow, The Brookings Institution; Joan Hoff-Wilson, Professor of History, Indiana University; Norman E. Saul, History Chair, University of Kansas. A number of other colleagues gave me their encouragement, suggestions, or support: John A. Armstrong, Professor Emeritus of Political Science, University of Wisconsin; Milton K. Barksdale, Librarian, Eastern Kentucky University; Robert F. Carberry, Dean of the College, Flagler College; Steven Evans, Business Administration Chair, Flagler College; Robert C. Frost, Director of Library Services, Flagler College; John L. Gaddis, Professor of History, Ohio University; Charles C. Hay, Archivist, Eastern Kentucky University; Robert L. Hungarland, Professor Emeritus of Business Administration, Eastern Kentucky University; John M. Long, Dean of the College of Arts and Humanities, Eastern Kentucky University; James R. Millar, Director of International Programs and Studies, University of Illinois; Michael J. Sherman, Social Science Chair, Flagler College. Additionally, I am indebted to Richard Dean Burns for his editorial services for this project as well as to my mentors and collaborators on earlier publications related to American-Soviet economic relations: George C. Herring, Professor of History, University of Kentucky; Joseph L. Wieczynski, Professor of History, Virginia Polytechnic Institute and State University.

Finally, several agencies graciously shared their facilities with me or promptly responded to my inquiries: Institute for American-Soviet Relations, Trade Representation of the USSR to the USA, U.S. Department of Agriculture, U.S. Department of Commerce, US-USSR Trade and Economic Council, and the libraries at the University of Florida and University of North Florida.

To Joyce's Mother, Wilma
And in loving memory of Joyce's Father, Orville

Contents

List of Tables

Introduction

PROBLEMS AND PROSPECTS

A detached observer of American-Soviet economic relations must wonder over the fact that these industrialized giants, the one noted for its romance with high technology and the other for its advocacy of scientific materialism, base their trade upon the exchange of minimally processed materials. Indeed, the Fall 1988 extension of the long-term grain agreement suggests that the annual transfer of nine million metric tons of U.S. grain to the U.S.S.R. will remain the main feature of their economic ties for the near future. On the one hand, this characteristic seems to mark a comfortably consistent pattern since it first appeared in the previous century when Russia was ruled by Tsars and America was innocent of world power. On the other hand, the circumstances as well as the types of farm products imported by Russia have certainly changed. Today, the Soviets view the need for American feed grain as a regrettable aberration, a temporary expedient designed to allay consumer demands for food. In reality, these imports expose serious flaws in the Soviet system—the limitations of a bureaucratized society and the shortcomings of a collectivized agriculture. The U.S. might well serve as a barometer for Soviet reforms. If such proposals as Mikhail Gorbachev's incentive team system succeed in agriculture, then *perestroika* in the Soviet Union will also promote a restructuring of American-Soviet commerce.

Meanwhile, the Soviets buy more than they sell in the U.S. market, a tradition that also transcends the Russian

Revolution. This imbalance highlights three interrelated issues that prevent an expansion beyond the $2-$3 billion annual turnover in American-Soviet trade: tariffs, currency, and financing. Since 1911, the U.S. government has used economic diplomacy, specifically the tariff, to protest Tsarist or Soviet policies. While the U.S.S.R. gained American most-favored-nation (MFN) tariff treatment in the 1930s, it lost this status during the Cold War. The Soviet Union subsequently introduced a double-column tariff in 1961 to punish the U.S. and any other nation withholding MFN treatment. Thus both countries have built economic barriers to normal commerce. Moreover, Soviet exports to the U.S. have been largely raw and semiprocessed materials such as ammonia, gold, nickel, platinum, potassium, and sable furskins. These goods are less affected by MFN because the American tariff increases relative to the degree of processing. The U.S. Trade Act of 1974 permitted the extension of MFN to the U.S.S.R. if it adheres to standards of free emigration stated in the Jackson-Vanik amendment. Since the Soviet Union prefers not to surrender its national sovereignty to the legislature of a foreign power, the tariff barriers are likely to remain in place.

The problems related to the imbalance in American-Soviet commerce are exacerbated by the fact that Soviet money, unlike the former gold-backed Tsarist currency, is internal and non-convertible except for the so-called "transferrable ruble" used in Comecon trade. An exchangeable currency is a Soviet goal. First, however, the U.S.S.R. must complete domestic price reforms and provide greater flexibility in the foreign trade monopoly. Second, the U.S. must end its opposition to Soviet interest in joining such international organizations as the General Agreement on Tariffs and Trade, World Bank, Asian Development Bank, and International Monetary Fund. An intricate series of difficult decisions, then, must be reached in Moscow and Washington before the Soviet Union can establish a convertible currency. The complexities of the situation indicate that, if this issue is to be resolved, it will take years of determined effort and good will on the part of both the Soviets and the Americans.

During the interim, the amount of economic interaction shared by the two countries is constrained by five financial factors: the Soviet ability to conclude barter agreements with U.S. companies, to use in America surplus convertible currency export earnings from other markets, to negotiate countertrade agreements that permit receipt of U.S. equipment for future Soviet exports manufactured with this equipment, to raise capital from Western and Japanese sources, and to secure U.S. trade credits and funds. The latter has posed difficulties for both Tsarist and Soviet Russia. Since 1917, the U.S. has generally denied long-term loans to the U.S.S.R. for ideological and economic reasons. For example, the Soviet Union has violated American debt law by refusing to honor the estimated $192 million borrowed in the U.S. by Imperial Russia. Moreover, the Stevenson amendment passed concurrently with the 1974 Trade Act limits to $300 million the amount of governmental credits available to the U.S.S.R. through the Export-Import Bank. The Soviet Union, though, possesses a high international credit rating and, unlike the U.S., is not a debtor nation. The country pays its bills, abounds in resources, and holds its repayments on debts to under 20% of its total convertible currency receipts. In January 1989, the U.S. State Department announced that Soviet officials had entered negotiations to settle Tsarist loans. If the talks are successful, the Soviets will be eligible for long-term loans from American banks, opening the possibility of an expansion in Soviet purchases of American products.

But what will the Americans permit the Russians to buy? The question would have been considered silly by U.S. entrepreneurs of an earlier age who relished the chance to take advantage of America's technological superiority to sell the Russians such goods as farm equipment and sewing machines. Times have changed. The year 1989 marked the fortieth anniversary of Congressionally mandated trade controls that allow the U.S. government to tell American businesses what they may or may not sell to the Soviet Union or to other nations. Export licenses have been used to protect America's national security, advance U.S. foreign policy goals, and support domestic economic interests. Proponents of strong controls claim that they impair the Soviet effort to enhance its military, while advocates of weaker restrictions argue that controls reduce America's competitiveness in the world market. In schizoid fashion, both views were elevated to national policy when President Reagan signed into law the Omnibus Trade and Competitiveness Act on August 23, 1988. It amends the Export Administration Act (EAA) of 1979, the current authority for controlling U.S. exports.

The new trade bill in equal measure reduces the "disincentives" to exports and strengthens enforcement of export controls. It proposes a license-free zone among those countries that maintain cooperative export control agreements with the U.S., i.e., nations prohibiting the export or reexport of embargoed goods. It also reduces the size and complexity of the commodity control list of those products denied the Soviet Union and its allies. And it redefines "foreign availability" and provides for the decontrol of those goods obtainable by the Soviets in the world market. On the other hand, the bill authorizes the Secretary of Commerce to withhold export licenses from individuals and companies in noncompliance with EAA regulations. It applies economic sanctions against Toshiba Corporation and Kongsberg Vaapenfabrikk for selling the Soviets forbidden technologies. And it defines sanctions to be used against future violators. The operative principle running throughout the legislation is America's ability to coordinate trade policy with her allies, a principle not easily kept as seen in past experience. Nevertheless, the bill is likely to result in a gradual increase in the types of American goods which can be sold to the U.S.S.R. during the 1990s.

While the U.S. has built a multi-tiered wall of regulations to stem the flow of strategic products, the U.S.S.R. has constructed a three-chambered fortress that impedes the entrance of U.S. and Western goods. First, 55% to 60% of Soviet foreign trade is tied to socialist allies via a complex network of more than a thousand bilateral and multilateral agreements. Since some of this trade is political in nature and often involves long-term barter arrangements, it is difficult to predict those conditions under which the Soviets might be willing or able to alter substantially its present commitment for the benefit of future commerce with non-socialist nations, including the U.S. Second, the U.S.S.R. has a centrally-planned economy where government officials, not the marketplace, determine product choice and quantity. Third, the country maintains a government monopoly over foreign trade. Some changes in the latter two characteristics emerged in the last half of the 1980s, among others: Soviet firms have been encouraged to be more responsive and accountable to market forces, individuals may legally establish their own businesses in certain economic sectors, the Ministry of Foreign Trade lost its exclusive control over foreign trade decisions, and the U.S.S.R. has urged U.S. and Western firms to form joint companies with Soviet enterprises. Whether the reforms succeed and whether the current Soviet leadership will continue (or be able to continue) these reforms is open to question. The opportunities today, however, for American participation in the Soviet economy are documentably as good and arguably better than at any time since the founding of the Soviet state.

Chapter 1

AMERICAN-RUSSIAN ECONOMIC RELATIONS, 1783-1917

During the American revolution, the British compounded their problems in North America by antagonizing most of Europe. Many reasons explain her partly self-imposed predicament including her behavior on the high seas. Naval supremacy allowed the British to board any ship they chose and declare as contraband any product that suited their purpose. And the British showed little restraint in exercising this power. For this, and other reasons, France, Spain, and Holland separately or in alliance joined the fledgling United States in warring with Britain. The British also applied their right of search and liberal notions of contraband to vessels in the Baltic Sea, offending Denmark-Norway, Russia, and Sweden. Under the leadership of Empress Catherine II (1762-1796) of Russia, the three countries signed mutual treaties (July 1780) upholding freedom of the seas and forming the Armed Neutrality. Within a few years, the Holy Roman Empire, Portugal, Prussia, and the Two Sicilies joined Catherine's league.

FRANCIS DANA AND THE FALSE BEGINNING

Some contemporaries correctly assessed the league's strength by referring to the "Armed Nullity" as a "sublime bubble."[1] Nevertheless, it distressed the British and inspired her enemies, especially the Americans. The Continental Congress decided in December to send a minister to Catherine and capitalize on her squabbles with Britain; however, the Americans failed to learn beforehand whether the Russians wanted to receive a U.S. representative. Instead, Congress naively expected the government there to welcome the arrival of any American diplomat.

Massachusetts lawyer, Francis Dana, received notice of his Congressional appointment in 1781. The former legislator and future justice resided in Paris where he assisted Benjamin Franklin and John Adams in maintaining ties with France, the only country that had officially recognized U.S. independence. Three ambassadors at one post seemed extravagant so Congress sent Adams to Holland and Dana to Russia. Dana and his young secretary, John Quincy Adams, set out for St. Petersburg and arrived in the Russian capital at the end of August.

Dana's mission was a personal and diplomatic disaster. He would never meet Catherine and rarely conversed with members of her Foreign Ministry, as the court virtually ignored his presence. For two years Dana secluded himself in his hotel room, suffering spells of pneumonia and ptomaine poisoning, writing letters of complaint to Adams in Holland, and practicing French by conversing with his secretary. His miserable existence must be blamed on Congress for saddling him with an impossible mission: to gain American entrance to the Armed Neutrality, to secure Russian recognition of the U.S., and to negotiate a commercial treaty. Logically, Catherine's neutral league could not admit a belligerent. The Empress dared not offer recognition to the American rebels because of her ambitions of being the mediatrix in Britain's disputes. Without recognition, a formal trade agreement was theoretically difficult if not impossible.[2]

FROM COMMERCE TO DIPLOMACY, 1783-1809

Dana left Russia on 16 August 1783. Two weeks later, Britain signed a peace treaty that acknowledged the independence of her former American colonies. If Dana had remained in St. Petersburg longer, the British barrier to his mission's success might have been lowered. As it was, Great Britain became the catalyst in American-Russian relations keeping the countries diplomatically apart in 1783 and bringing them together in 1809. During the interim, despite Dana's failures, American-Russian economic ties grew in strength and number throughout the 25-year period.

In the eighteenth century, the tsars ruled over the greatest industrial power on Earth. Russia produced high quality flax and hemp and more and better iron than Great Britain. This fact seems all the more remarkable because Tsarist Russia evokes an image of backwardness—and for good reason. Society was oppressed, millions of peasants were enslaved as serfs, and the rulers were not hampered by the niceties of a constitution. Russia later squandered her lead in the nascent Industrial Revolution by failing to adapt to changing conditions.

The U.S. economy depended on certain Russian products. Hemp was used for rope, flax for sail, iron for anchors, bracings and nails, and all these items were vital for ships. In an age before trains and interstate highways, ships carried not only America's foreign commerce but most domestic trade as well. While a colony, America acquired these important supplies via British ships; though Boston, New York, and Philadelphia merchants occasionally sent ships to the Baltic in defiance of British law. Independence enabled America to trade directly with Russia. The first two ships flying a U.S. flag arrived in St. Petersburg the same year Dana's mission ended and by 1797, a 100 American vessels visited Russia.

The Russian-American pattern of trade found U.S. vessels sailing to the West Indies and picking up sugar, indigo, rice, and rum. They traveled across the Atlantic and into the North and Baltic Seas and sold these prized articles to Denmark, Sweden, and Prussia. The ships then carried money or letters of credit to St. Petersburg where the captains and bursars purchased hemp, linen, and iron as well as candles and tallow (animal fats used for soap, lamps, and lubricants). Loaded with Russian products, the ships journeyed to America, selling part of their cargos in New England and taking the rest to the West Indies to start the process all over again. An example of the mutual benefits drawn from this commerce came when Tripoli pirates captured an American ship in 1803, and Tsar Alexander I (1801-1825) sought to secure the release of the vessel.

In 1803, U.S. Secretary of State James Madison appointed Levett Harris, an American merchant, to serve as a consul in St. Petersburg. Shortly thereafter, the Tsar and U.S. President Thomas Jefferson established a personal correspondence. European conflicts only strengthened these close ties. The fallout from the French Revolution engulfed the continent in war, with few intermissions, from 1792 to 1815. During the ensuing economic warfare, British Orders in Council and Napoleon's Berlin and Milan Decrees mutually prohibited trade between Great Britain and the continent. American and neutral shipping suffered the consequences. On 22 December 1807, Jefferson signed the Embargo Act into law. American trade with Great Britain, France or their allies became illegal. U.S. merchants avoided economic suicide by violating the letter and spirit of the law. One of their more creative solutions was to keep some of their ships out of American harbors. These vessels illegally plied the waters between warring nations. An important trade pattern connected Great Britain and Russia, and American ships carried the goods. The British needed Russian naval stores to maintain their fleets, and the Russians wanted the sugar, coffee, and cotton normally acquired via British ships. Enterprising American captains negotiated in London for smuggling licenses that protected their ships from British men-of-war. And the Russians closed their eyes to the fake papers carried by U.S. captains, papers indicating that their ships had sailed from America or a country under French control. Despite the U.S. embargo, British orders, and French decrees, over 200 American vessels annually dropped anchor in Russian ports after 1808. They carried such an abundance of cargo that by 1811 Russian prices for British goods actually dropped 20%, and this at a time when each nation had technically banned trade with the other.[3]

Neutral America had become downright crucial to Russia in time of war. Under these circumstances Tsar Alexander issued an imperial ukase (order) in June 1808, appointing Andrei Dashkov to the posts of consul-general in Philadelphia and charge d'affaires at Congress. The College (Ministry) of Foreign Affairs instructed Dashkov to focus all his energies on "the achievement of one aim only—to encourage active and direct trade between the two countries."[4] Dashkov made trade the central subject of his first conversation with newly elected President, James Madison. Fearful that recognition of Russia might somehow drag America into Europe's wars, the U.S. Senate turned down one candidate and delayed until 1809 approving Dana's former secretary, John Quincy Adams, as America's envoy to Russia. Adams reached St. Petersburg in October. Indicative of the era's perils, warships of several nations stopped his ship, the *Horace*, a total of 11 times during the single voyage. His arrival completed the exchange of representatives and marked the opening of official relations.

WAR AND PEACE AND THE POLITICS OF COMMERCE

Russia's subversion of the French Continental System angered Napoleon, and Britain's harassment of unlicensed U.S. shipping aggravated Americans. On 18 June 1812,

America declared war on Great Britain and, four days later, France invaded Russian territory. Ironically, the U.S. surrendered its neutral status at the very moment the English and Russians had joined hands as allies in a common struggle against France. Moreover, two days before the U.S. became a belligerent, the British government announced to the House of Commons that the Orders in Council—the orders directing the British navy to seize neutral vessels on their way to the continent—no longer applied to American ships. If the radio or the telegraph had existed in 1812 the U.S.probably would not have engaged Great Britain in war.

When the conflict began, a convoy of 40 American ships left England for Russia under the protection of British men-of-war. New England merchants worried about Britain's change of role from guardian to warden of American ships. The merchants sent several fast ships to Europe to warn as many U.S. captains as possible before official word of America's declaration of war reached London. One schooner, the *Champlin*, caught up with the convoy in Gothenburg, Sweden, in time to allow the American ships to slip away unchallenged and sail for Kronstadt, island port-of-call for St. Petersburg. A few ships remained in Russian waters but most completed their voyages once captains realized that the enemy would honor its licenses, war or no war. The U.S. government was not so charitable. It sent privateers to Northern Europe to prey upon English vessels trading with Russia through the port of Arkhangel'sk.[5]

In 1813, three of these privateers managed to capture 24 British ships, seriously disrupting Russo-British commerce. It was the type of activity Alexander wanted to avoid since his break with Napoleon made Russia eligible for direct trade with England. Shortly after Moscow fell to Napoleon's Grand Army, a Pyrrhic victory that led to Bonaparte's ultimate defeat, Alexander offered himself as a mediator in the Anglo-American conflict. Great Britain turned down the Tsar's offer, indirectly acknowledging Russia's favorable attitude toward the U.S. Nevertheless, the British agreed to direct negotiations with U.S. representatives in the Netherlands where the Treaty of Ghent was signed in 1814.[6]

THE TALE OF TWO TREATIES

Shortly before the Americans and British signed this agreement, a coalition of nations defeated Napoleon and occupied Paris. The end to Europe's strife enabled commerce to resume its normal course, including the carrying trade that connected Russia, the U.S., and the West Indies. When this triangular commerce first appeared after the American Revolution, New England merchants had also begun sending ships to China. The favored trade pattern that evolved found U.S. ships dropping anchor in Russian-America, bartering guns and rum for Alaskan furs, and transporting the furs to China where they were exchanged for tea, spices, and silks. When ships ladened with these goods finally returned to U.S. ports, they brought enormous wealth to the merchants who saved a small percent of their profits to buy cheap weapons and spirits, starting the process again.

Muskets and rum proved to be a deadly combination in the hands of such belligerent tribes as the Tlingets who used American weapons to kill hundreds of Russians between 1790 and 1822. When not engaged in destructive commerce, the Americans brawled with the natives, defiled their women, and killed the Indians' sources of food. The view of the Russian-American Company was that the uncouth and uncontrollable Yankees threatened Russian-America's very existence. Europe's conflicts had allowed the U.S. to dominate the coastal fur trade and when the fighting ended, this dominance continued. In September 1821, Tsar Alexander took two steps to preserve the peace and integrity of Russia's American territory. First, in renewing the Russian-American Company's charter he gave the Imperial Navy a role in the company's administration. Second, he issued a ukase expanding Russia's boundary in North America from 54' 40" to 51' latitude (just north of the present State of Washington). The ukase also forbid foreigners from stepping foot on Russian-American soil and their ships from aproaching within 100 miles of land.

Word of these drastic prescripts naturally raised cries of anguish in New England. Alexander had done more than upset a few merchants and seamen. He had tried to redefine the meaning of territorial waters and deny U.S. claims to the Oregon territory. As a result, Secretary of State John Quincy Adams made it clear that the U.S. would not acknowledge the validity of the Tsar's ukase, and he initiated negotiations to modify its contents. In the midst of these discussions, President James Monroe issued his famous declaration asserting the noncolonization principle for the Western Hemisphere. Numerous factors involving foreign as well as domestic politics led to the Monroe Doctrine (1823), including Russia's arbitrary expansion of her boundaries. Ironically, the Russian-American Company joined the U.S. in criticizing the Tsar's action. It wanted help in controlling, not eliminating the Americans. Besides destructive articles, Yankee captains brought in food and other necessities and conducted most of the company's fur trade with China. Once Alexander's ukase went into effect in 1822, annual dividends for Russian stockholders plummeted to zero from a high of 155 rubles per share in 1819.

A group of stockholders petitioned the Russian government to revise its policy. This internal pressure made Russia amenable to negotiations and resulted in the first American-Russian treaty, signed in St. Petersburg on 17 April 1824. It reestablished the former boundary at 54' 40" and permitted virtually open U.S. access to both the territorial waters and shoreline of Russian-America. In return for these concessions, the U.S. promised to exempt liquors, firearms, and gunpowder as articles of commerce in the fur trade with the indians. With this generous treaty the Imperial government had made a conscious decision to curry American favor, a foreign policy position it maintained for decades.

The Russian Empire realistically appraised its position in the Pacific Northwest relative to the U.S. Several nations contested the area. Spain, for example, held claim as far north as 61' latitude, i.e., to the southern edge of the Yukon. Russia, however, understood that the region would ultimately fall to one or both of two nations, Great Britain and the United States. And the Imperial government expected that the U.S. would win the territorial struggle. This pro-American stance grew from the *Realpolitik* notion that the U.S. posed no threat to the Empire except in North America where Russia's holdings were both fragile and comparatively unimportant. On the other hand, Great Britain challenged Russian interests in North America, in China, across Central Asia, through the eastern Mediterranean and into Europe. The threat of war overshadowed Russo-British relations during the bulk of the nineteenth century. Coupled with the inferior condition of Russia's merchant marine, this caused the Imperial government to desire U.S. ships as an alternative to British ships that carried most of Russia's foreign trade.

Events in Europe and the eastern Mediterranean soon reinforced Russia's benign attitude toward America. In 1830, Belgium sought independence from the Netherlands and Great Britain functioned as Belgium's protector. The liberal uprisings across the continent shocked Tsar Nicholas I (1825-1855) who promoted autocracy, nationality, and orthodoxy in Russia and legitimacy in Europe. At the same time, after centuries of struggle, Russia secured from the Ottoman Empire the permanent right of commercial passage through the Dardanelles and Bosporus Straits. The Treaty of Adrianople (1829) opened the Black Sea to Russian trade and converted the Ukrainian city of Odessa into a major international port. If conflict erupted between Russia and Britain, St. Petersburg wanted U.S. vessels carrying its Black Sea commerce.

When James Buchanan, U.S. minister to Russia, handed his credentials to the Imperial government on 11 June 1832, Nicholas still debated using force to restore Belgium to the Netherlands. Buchanan made, like all his predecessors, a *pro forma* request for a treaty to normalize American-Russian trade relations. His petition was accepted with unaccustomed alacrity, and a few months later he signed a Commercial Treaty. Ratified by the U.S. Senate in May 1833, it remained in effect until 1913. The document contained 13 articles including such provisions as most-favored-nation tariff treatment, reciprocity in pilot and lighthouse fees, and protection for the property of foreign nationals. It strengthened the economic bonds that linked the nations. U.S. shipping could aid Russia in time of war and Russia could serve as a potential counterweight to the threat posed by Britain and France to American interests in the Western Hemisphere.[7]

THE POLITICAL LEGACY OF FRIENDSHIP

A Russo-British war did not erupt until 1854 and American fears of British or French intervention in the New World did not materialize until the U.S. Civil War. The latter opened the opportunity for France to try (1863-1867) carving out an empire at the expense of Mexico. The harmonious relations illustrated by the Commercial Treaty lasted for decades and served America and Russia well in times of national crisis. During Russia's disastrous Crimean War (1854-1856) with Britain, France, and Turkey, the U.S. remained a most benevolent neutral. And when civil conflict threatened America's existence, the regime of Tsar Alexander II (1855-1881) supported the Union cause and ignored the South's representatives. Moreover, Russia helped nullify the French plan to force a six-month truce on the warring American states which might have destroyed the Union and assisted French ambitions in Mexico.

The vital role Russia played as America's champion in Europe prompted President Abraham Lincoln to overlook Russia's shortcomings and ideological differences. In 1863, Russia brutally suppressed a Polish uprising but the U.S. refused to join the European powers in condemning the autocratic Imperial government. When events in Poland nearly ignited a European war, the U.S. aided Russia by harboring elements of its Far East and Baltic squadrons in San Francisco and New York during the winter of 1863-1864. The fleets ostensibly arrived as a sign of Russia's support for the Union; however, the ships would be available in case of a European war as commerce raiders against British or French merchantmen.

The congruence of political purpose of the two nations found expression in the sale of Russian America to the U.S. in 1867. Not only was Russian America a financial liability, but Tsar Alexander and his advisers thought the sale would cement Russo-American ties and lead to a formal military alliance against Great Britain. These notions vanished when the U.S. and Great Britain settled contentious issues in the Washington Treaty of 1871. At the same time, Russia moved away from her traditional allies in Central Europe and toward detente with her former foes. In 1907 Russia signed a treaty with Great Britain linking her with France in the Triple Entente.

Once Great Britain was no longer an adversary common to America and Russia, their shared political activities sharply dropped. This decline permitted other elements, those accentuating differences, to emerge and claim center stage. Many Americans were alarmed that Tsars Alexander III (1881-1894) and Nicholas II (1894-1917) tacitly sanctioned anti-Jewish pogroms. Immediate reminders of tsarist persecution could be found in America as tens of thousands of Russian immigrants annually crowded Ellis Island on their journey to freedon. Finally, America and Russia became competitors in the Far East especially after the U.S. conquered a Pacific Empire from Spain. When

Russia's expansion into Manchuria led to war with Japan (1904-1905), the U.S. tended to favor a Japanese victory. Nevertheless, the legacy of American-Russian friendship remained strong enough for the U.S. to serve as a mediator in negotiating peace between Russia and Japan at Portsmouth, New Hampshire, in 1905.[8]

TABLE 1

U.S. Trade with Russia			
(In Dollar Amounts)			
Year	Imports	Exports	Total	As % of U.S. Trade
1822	3,307,028	529,081	3,836,109	2.69
1832	3,248,852	500,629	3,749,481	2.15
1842	1,350,106	831,615	2,181,721	1.12
1852	1,581,620	1,200,480	2,782,100	0.75
1862	595,202	57,032	652,234	0.18
1872	1,965,393	6,921,785	8,887,178	0.80
1882	2,473,730	11,463,151	13,936,881	0.94
1892	4,926,630	6,698,835	11,625,465	0.62
1902	7,342,586	10,332,579	17,675,165	0.77
1912	22,110,500	22,722,488	44,832,988	1.16
1913	29,315,217	26,465,214	55,780,431	1.30
1914	23,320,157	31,303,149	54,623,306	1.28
1915	3,394,040	60,827,531	64,221,571	1.44
1916	6,916,844	310,242,890	317,159,734	4.85
1917	9,464,264	558,894,445	568,358,709	6.35

Adapted from: U.S. Treasury Department. *Statistical Tables Exhibiting the Commerce of the United States with European Countries from 1790 to 1890*. Washington, DC: GPO, 1893; U.S. Commerce Department. *Foreign Commerce and Navigation of the United States*. Washington, DC: GPO, Annual.

ECONOMIC RELATIONS TO 1914

What relations remained between Russia and America after the sale of Alaska focused almost exclusively on the economic realm. Between 1868 and 1884, the countries modified the Commercial Treaty by adding several articles pertaining to trademarks and navigation fees, and in 1894 they signed an executive agreement on sealing in the North Pacific. Despite the intent of both governments to nurture commerce, trade statistics indicate that the promise of close economic ties went largely unfulfilled. The turnover (exports and imports) in America's trade with Russia totaled $3.7 million in 1832. Fifty years later it stood at $13.9 million; yet in the same period U.S. trade world-wide jumped from $176 million to nearly $1.5 billion. The relative importance of Russia as an American trading partner declined by over 50% during the middle half of the nineteenth century. And from 1882 to 1914 trade with Russia hovered around a paltry 1% of America's total foreign commerce.

Technological advances partly explain the small amount of economic activity conducted between the two nations. As the U.S. developed its natural resources and as the materials and mode of power for ships changed, Russian products no longer played a significant role in the American economy. Also throughout the nineteenth century, the American merchant fleet experienced a gradual erosion in its status. In 1810 the gross tonnage of U.S. ships engaged in foreign commerce was actually 52,000 tons higher than in 1912. By 1914 vessels registered to nations other than the U.S. transported a whopping 90.3% of its trade. Not only did America lose its merchant shipping but, like Russia, had become dependent on other countries for carrying its international commerce.

American and Russian reliance on foreign merchant fleets illustrated one of several parallels in their economic development. Another similarity was the assimilation and exploitation of their hinterlands, the American West and

Russian Siberia, which absorbed a significant amount of their national energies during the nineteenth century. Additionally, both countries experienced rapid industrialization, with all the attendant benefits and ills. Russia established the gold standard in 1897 as a means of attracting European investment,while the U.S. resisted domestic political demands to mint silver and kept the integrity of its gold-based currency. And both nations built economic barriers to safeguard their home manufactures. Between 1877 and 1891 the Imperial government revised import duties upward until Russia possessed the highest tariff in Europe. At the same time the U.S. moved to strident protectionism culminating in the McKinley Tariff (1890) which added on average 49.5% to the cost of imported manufactures. Finally, Russia and America retained an agrarian base and the bulk of their exports, even to each other, were agricultural in nature. Russia exchanged hides, wool, fur, and flax for U.S. cotton.

Ironically, some of the very similarities that restricted the interaction between the countries also gave rise to the greatest optimism for the future of their economic relations. The U.S. was years ahead of Russia in communications and transportation as well as mechanized agriculture. Russians could draw from America's advanced experience in these areas, while U.S. businessmen hoped for large sales in the Russian market. For example, Russia employed a number of Americans in establishing the Empire's telegraph system. Three decades after the U.S.'s first transcontinental railroad, the Imperial government finished its Trans-Siberian line in 1903. The Russians spanned Siberia's numerous rivers with American-style bridges and operated many of their trains with U.S.-built Baldwin locomotives and Westinghouse brakes. Of manufactured products, the most significant U.S. export to Russia was harvesting machinery such as binders, reapers, mowers, and rakes. The McCormick (International Harvester) brand alone annually attracted over 10,000 Russian buyers after 1900.

Sales of these and other U.S. products would have been greater had it not been for Russia's prohibitive tariff. Some enterprising Americans circumvented the Empire's high import duties by investing directly in Russia. The most prosperous was the Singer Manufacturing Company which incorporated a branch firm under Imperial law in 1897 and built a plant near Podolsk in 1900. Within a decade Singer possessed a near monopoly on the manufacture and sale of sewing machines in Russia. No other U.S. company matched Singer's success, but a number of well-known American firms established Russian subsidiaries to provide services or make products ranging from life insurance to pharmaceutics. Moreover, by 1911, Russia had garnered a respectable 8% of America's total foreign investment.

While Americans found ways to thwart Russia's tariff, they had difficulty overcoming Russia's reliance on intermediaries. As the U.S. merchant fleet declined in the nineteenth century, products exchanged by Russia and America were transported on foreign vessels and frequently transshipped from other countries especially England and Germany. Exporters in New York or St. Petersburg often consigned goods for resale to foreign nationals in, for example, Liverpool or Hamburg, thereby wreaking havoc with statistics on American-Russian trade. Once U.S. products finally reached Russian soil, they were generally in the hands of German trading houses which knew the Russians and their needs and offered generous credit terms to local retailers. They gave preference to cheap German or English manufactures because U.S. products, though frequently better built, were too costly in the protected Russian market. Only such American companies as International Harvester took the trouble to investigate the Russian market, establish credit facilities, and create regional sales and service centers to deal directly with Russian buyers.

In their attempt to avoid intermediaries, U.S. firms employed as their agents Russian immigrants and naturalized Americans who understood the language and culture. Many of the agents they hired were Jews. While the Commercial Treaty extended the Empire's legal protection to American nationals, it afforded few safeguards to American Jews, native or naturalized, because Russian law sanctioned anti-Semitism. The Imperial government's ill treatment of American Jews had been a festering issue since the 1870s. By the early 1900s, news of infamous anti-Jewish pogroms in Russia coupled with the growing number of reports of indignities endured by American Jews working or visiting in Russia raised a public outcry. In 1911, Congress forced the Taft Administration to express U.S. concern by abrogating the Commercial Treaty, effective on 1 January 1913.

A public interest group, in this case American Jews, proved influential in changing American foreign policy—a precedent for the twentieth century. Moreover, the incident foreshadowed the practice of using economic diplomacy to achieve political goals. The U.S. government essentially challenged the internal affairs of a European nation. Meanwhile, the U.S. had helped neither American nor Russian Jews whose position in Russia deteriorated in the adverse publicity generated by the controversy. Because of an informal agreement reached by those Russian and American officials opposed to the treaty's abrogation, its demise had no effect on commerce. In fact, within a few years, American-Russian trade increased ten-fold to become a prominent feature in the economic life of both countries.[9]

WORLD WAR I

In the summer of 1914, the Great War began in Europe and caused the unusual rise in American-Russian economic activity. The Allies, principally composed of France, Great Britain, Japan, and Russia (later, Italy) battled Germany and Austria-Hungary (later, the Ottoman Empire). America avoided entering the conflict until April 1917, but because geography and sentiment favored the Allies, the U.S. eventually supplied funds and goods to these countries long before she joined them in combat as an Associate Power. Germany, though, held the key for understanding the dramatic shift in American-Russian economic relations. In 1913, America accounted for 5.8% of Russia's imports, Germany for 47.4%. Several years later when German products could not legally cross the Empire's borders, nearly 40% of Russia's imports came from the U.S. as America filled the economic vacuum created by Russia's belligerency with Germany.

Wartime geography explains why the U.S. was the beneficiary of the abrupt change in the pattern of Russia's foreign trade. The German navy soon controlled the Baltic, and the Turks closed the Straits to the Black Sea after they joined the Central Powers in the autumn of 1914. Within months, all of European Russia's ports-of-entry were useless except for Arkhangel'sk which ice shut down during winter months. Thus Vladivostok, located by the Pacific Ocean and at the terminus for the Trans-Siberian Railroad, stood as a gateway to Russia for U.S. products shipped from San Francisco or Seattle.

The ease in shipping goods from West Coast America to Russian Siberia was in sharp contrast to the difficulties encountered in financing the sales. Russia exported approximately $20 million worth of goods to the U.S. and imported nearly $1 billion in American products. The Empire needed to rectify the huge trade deficit with money from other sources, primarily loans. Wilson's adminstration initially complicated this process by banning private U.S. loans to all belligerents as part of its definition of neutrality. When the ban threatened war-related commerce and, hence, American prosperity it was lifted in 1915, but with mixed results for Russia. The normally small amount of American-Russian trade meant that neither country had established adequate banking facilities in its counterpart to handle all the activity generated by the war. Moreover, U.S. bankers shied away from buying or selling Imperial government bonds because Russia, unlike other European powers, lacked domestic American assets that might be used for collateral. The Empire finally secured $233 million in private U.S. funds, a sizable sum but not nearly enough to counter the deficit. Russia's war-time partners, France and Great Britain, supplied the balance by turning over to the Empire 70% of the $2.1 billion they had raised in U.S. loans. From one perspective, then, American money paid for American goods sent to Russia.

Russia used the capital to buy a wide assortment of war materiel in America, ranging from automobiles to wire. Combat supplies occupied most of the available shipping space and forced the Tsarist government to restrict private imports. These restrictions disrupted the trade in various peacetime commodities. U.S. typewriters, for example, virtually ceased to enter Russia a year after achieving sales in excess of a million dollars in 1914. More distressing was the 90% drop in cotton and agricultural machinery. Russian industry failed to meet the demand for agricultural implements, crucial for efficient food production. Similarly, the amount of cotton grown in Turkestan and Transcaucasia did not meet wartime requirements. The Imperial government gradually adjusted its priorities and recognized that food and clothing were as vital to the Russian army as guns and ammunition. By 1916, U.S. cotton exports to Russia matched pre-war levels and sales of agricultural machinery rebounded to $3.6 million from $0.7 million the previous year.

The war resulted in Russia buying more U.S. goods in three years than in the previous century. The purchases created an American corporate interest in Russian commerce that found expression in the incorporation early in 1916 of the American-Russian Chamber of Commerce. As an outgrowth of a Moscow-based group of Russian merchants and importers, the chamber attracted members from among America's leading industrial and financial firms such as United States Steel, Westinghouse, National City Bank, Chase National Bank, and International Harvester. Headquartered in New York City, the chamber gave organization to American business concern for Russia by holding meetings, planning expositions, sending representatives to Russia, providing translation services, and preparing literature on American industry for Russian entrepreneurs. The newly-founded chamber also embodied American optimism that the unusual trade activity would continue unabated at the conclusion of hostilities. Most importantly, it seemed guaranteed that the U.S. would permanently replace Germany as one of the leading promoters and benefactors in Russian development.[10]

* * * * * *

On the eve of the Russian Revolution certain enduring traits had emerged in American-Russian economic relations, characteristics that would transcend abrupt political changes and continue into the Soviet period. First, third-party nations influenced the scope and amount of American-Russian interaction. Second, agriculturally-related products formed the backbone of the trade shared by the two countries. Third, America and Russia experienced similar aspects in their economic development, but Russia lagged behind the U.S. which made America more significant to the material progress of Russia. Fourth, the importance of U.S. goods and technology to Russia contributed to an imbalance in their trade that favored America. Fifth, Russia needed funds outside the matrix of American-Russian commerce to pay the difference between its sales and purchases. Sixth, the U.S. government showed a willingness to use America's economic advantage over Russia to achieve political ends. Finally, the rise and fall in politics failed to correspond to the rise and fall in economics. From 1914 to 1917, the nadir in political ties perversely accompanied the pinnacle in American-Russian economic relations.

NOTES

1. John Adams used the "sublime bubble" label, and Catherine II described her own creation as the "Armed Nullity." See Thomas A. Bailey, *A Diplomatic History of the American People* (New York: Appleton-Century-Crofts, 1964), 40.

2. W. P. Cresson, *Francis Dana: A Puritan Diplomat at the Court of Catherine the Great* (New York: Dial, 1930), 129-303; David M. Griffiths, "Nikita Panin, Russian Diplomacy, and the American Revolution," *Slavic Review* 28 (March 1969), 1-24. See also Gladys Scott Thompson, *Catherine the Great and the Expansion of Russia* (New York: Macmillan, 1947).

3. Alfred W. Crosby, Jr., *America, Russia, Hemp, and Napoleon: American Trade with Russia and the Baltic, 1783-1812* (Columbus: Ohio State University Press, 1965), 198-225; J. William Frederichson, "American Shipping in the Trade with Northern Europe, 1783-1880," *Scandinavian Economic History Review* 4 (1956), 110-125.

4. Quote from Nikolai N. Bolkhovitinov, *The Beginnings of Russian-American Relations, 1775-1815* (Cambridge: Harvard University Press, 1975), 198. See also John C. Hildt, *Early Negotiations of the U.S. with Russia* (Baltimore: Johns Hopkins University Press, 1906).

5. Crosby, *America, Russia, Hemp, and Napoleon*, 247-262.

6. Patrick C. T. White, *A Nation on Trial: America and the War of 1812* (New York: Wiley, 1967), 138-145. See also reprint of Charles F. Adams, ed., *John Quincy Adams in Russia, Comprising Portions of the Diary of John Quincy Adams from 1809 to 1814* (New York: Praeger, 1970).

7. Philip Shriver Klein, *President James Buchanan: A Biography* (University Park: Pennsylvania State University Press, 1962), 78-94; Howard I. Kushner, *Conflict on the Northwest Coast: American-Russian Rivalry in the Pacific Northwest, 1790-1867* (Westport: Greenwood, 1975), 43-62. See also James R. Gibson, *Imperial Russia In Frontier America: The Changing Geography of Supply of Russian America, 1784-1867* (New York: Oxford University Press, 1976); Semen B. Okun', *Rossiisko-amerikanskaia*

kompaniia (Moscow: Sotsekiz, 1939); Dexter Perkins, *A History of the Monroe Doctrine* (Boston: Little, Brown, 1963).

8. Eugene P. Trani, *The Treaty of Portsmouth: An Adventure in American Diplomacy* (Lexington: University of Kentucky Press, 1969), 46-61. See also Ronald J. Jenson, *The Alaskan Purchase and Russian-American Relations* (Seattle: University of Washington Press, 1975); M. M. Malkin, *Grazhdanskaia voina v SShA i tsarskaia Rossiia* (Moscow: Ogiz, 1939); Edward H. Zabriskie, *American-Russian Rivalry in the Far East: A Study in Diplomacy and Power Politics, 1895-1914* (Philadelphia: University of Pennsylvania Press, 1946).

9. Ann E. Healy, "Tsarist Anti-Semitism and Russian-American Relations," *Slavic Review* 42 (Fall 1983), 408-425; Gilbert Charles Kohlenberg, "Russian-American Economic Relations, 1906-1917" (Ph.D. Diss., University of Illinois, 1951), 90-127; George Sherman Queen, "The United States and the Material Advance in Russia, 1881-1906" (Ph.D. Diss., University of Illinois, 1941), 219-221.

10. Barbara Jackson Gaddis, "American Economic Interests in Russia: August, 1914-March, 1917" (M.A. Thesis, University of Texas, 1966), 102; John Lewis Gaddis, *Russia, the Soviet Union, and the United States: An Interpretive History* (New York: Wiley, 1978), 52. See also Benson Lee Grayson, *Russian-American Relations in World War I* (New York: Ungar, 1979).

Chapter 2

THE FALL AND RISE IN AMERICAN-SOVIET ECONOMIC RELATIONS

In the late winter of 1917, the Tsarist regime collapsed almost without struggle in a popular revolution ignited by bread and fuel shortages in Petrograd. On 12 March some members of the dissolved Duma (the state assembly with limited powers) met to appoint themselves and other public figures to a Provisional Government. The new administration was an interim body designed to keep things in some sort of running order until a convention could be called to fashion a permanent government. The new ministers, overly sensitive to their temporary status, deferred many decisions including such pressing issues as land reform and the status of national minorities.

Unfortunately for the Provisional Government, it overlooked Russia's catastrophic conditions to make the one choice guaranteed to bring its downfall: to continue the Empire's war with the Central Powers. This decision prompted American business and political leaders to invest the Provisional Government with nearly the same strengths and democratic virtues as its counterpart in Washington, DC. Nicholas II barely had time to abdicate before the American-Russian Chamber of Commerce cabled its congratulations to the new regime. Knowledge of the Provisional Government's policy meant that the half-billion dollars in annual U.S. sales to Russia would apparently continue for the war's duration. Moreover, "a liberal

Russia," the chamber concluded, "means a progressive Russia, and such a Russia will naturally turn toward the United States for assistance in the reorganization and reconstruction of its economic resources."[1] The Provisional Government's decision also gratified the Wilson Administration, but for a different reason. By ridding itself of autocracy, Russia had become a "fit partner" in Wilson's dream "to make the world safe for democracy." America, then, quickly extended diplomatic recognition to the Provisional Government—our "democratic" ally—and soon made available $450 million in credits and other forms of aid to help Russia continue fighting.

EFFECTS OF THE RUSSIAN REVOLUTION

Despite this aid and good will, the Provisional Government actually possessed little authority and prestige within Russia. Elected delegates representing the capital's workers and soldiers occupied the Duma building to establish a popular council or soviet. Soon to be imitated in many other towns and cities, the Petrograd Soviet exercised real power because it reflected the will of the majority. In fact, the Provisional Government had been created in consultation with the Soviet and bowed to its will on many matters. Since the official administration procrastinated in calling a Constituent Assembly and in dealing with Russia's severe problems, the dual system was rectified at the Provisional Government's expense and one of the more radical Marxist groups, the Bolsheviks (renamed Communists in 1918), served as the catalyst. On 7 November, ostensibly to protect a Congress of Soviets then meeting in the capital city, the Bolsheviks conducted a successful insurrection. They deposed the official regime and catapulted to power Vladimir I. Ulianov, better known by his pseudonym, Lenin.

With Lenin as chairman of the Council of People's Commissars, the new Soviet government angered many

Americans because it promptly sought a separate peace with the Central Powers. In truth, the country had unofficially withdrawn from the conflict months before the Bolshevik phase of the Revolution. Russia had suffered more than any other country during the war. Almost eight million soldiers had been killed, wounded, or taken prisoner while civilian losses in death, injury, dislocation, and property damage had reached such tragic proportions as to escape final count. Order Number One issued by the Petrograd Soviet on 14 March turned military units over to elected committees, undermining the officer corps and destroying the chain of command. Strikes and demonstrations closed factories and disrupted transportation, and food production fell as peasants conducted their own revolution against the landed aristocracy. Thousands of peasant-soldiers deserted their military posts to participate in the greatest confiscation of property in the history of the world. The movement was so strong that Communists dared not challenge the peasant land-grab until they collectivized agriculture more than a decade later. Meanwhile, the Eastern Front did not witness a serious military engagement after July 1917.

Few Americans fathomed the depths of Russia's collapse, but many recalled that Lenin and others had earlier received Germany's assistance in returning to Russia from their Swiss exile. U.S. leaders perceived the peace-seeking Bolsheviks as abettors of the German enemy. Russia's withdrawal from the war theoretically permitted Germany to transfer forces from the Eastern to the Western Front where American soldiers were engaging in combat. These circumstances led the Wilson Administration to refuse diplomatic recognition to the Soviet government, withdraw unspent ($262 million) credits, and clamp an embargo on Russian trade. The latter policy coincided with the Allied decision to add Russian territory to the general blockade against the Central Powers. Meanwhile, the Soviets nationalized industry and seized foreign property.

Added to the now worthless Russian war bonds, all U.S. investment in the former Empire vanished and with little hope of recovery. The Soviet government, compelled to move to Moscow because German troops threatened to capture Petrograd, signed a peace treaty with the Central Powers at Brest-Litovsk. The commercial arrangements attached to the treaty forced a renewal of German-Russian economic ties.

In a few months, America lost not only hundreds of millions of dollars in sales and investments but also its potential as the driving force in Russia's international commerce and internal development. The American-Russian Chamber of Commerce blamed this spectacular reversal on the Bolsheviks and became a strident anti-Soviet lobbying group. In July 1918, the U.S. joined several Allied nations in a military intervention of Russia, ostensibly to prevent Germany from seizing military supplies stockpiled at Russian ports. These forces, though, gave protection and sometimes overt assistance to those Russians struggling unsuccessfully to unseat the Soviet government in the brutal Civil War. When the Soviet government achieved victory in the Civil War, the chamber became a protective society for Americans who held Imperial government bonds. Its new role guaranteed its divorce from Soviet Russia.[2]

BEGINNINGS OF AMERICAN-SOVIET TRADE

At the end of the first year (1921) of American-Soviet trade, the total turnover in dollar amounts reached $16.9 million—less than a third of pre-war commercial activity. Decisions by the U.S. government after lifting the embargo hindered economic relations with Soviet Russia. For most of the 1920s, the Departments of State and Commerce issued warnings that discouraged or prohibited American industrialists and exporters from extending long-term credits to Soviet Russia, and bankers from sponsoring long-term loans or subscribing to long-term bonds to help finance trade. The U.S. Assay Office refused to accept Russian gold to pay for American goods because the Soviets had confiscated so much wealth it could not prove title to any gold, including bullion mined after 1917. Finally, the absence of diplomatic relations to 1933 created unacceptable risks for many American businessmen. There were no U.S. commercial agents and consuls in Soviet Russia to give assistance, nor were there trade agreements to provide protection. The classic example of this emerged during the strange interlude associated with Ludwig C. A. K. Martens, an appointed Soviet representative to America in 1919. Martens engaged numerous small U.S. firms in $30 million worth of contracts that were promised on an alteration in America's trade and recognition policies. When the U.S. State Department threatened to deport Martens in December 1920, he fled the country effectively nullifying the agreements.

Thus, the initiative in American-Soviet economic relations fell to the Soviets who were least able to promote them. War, Revolution, and Civil War had ruined and exhausted Russia. Also, Russia forfeited huge chunks of European territory: Bessarabia, Estonia, Finland, Latvia, and Lithuania plus the Polish provinces and portions of White Russia. The loss of these regions contributed to the 80% drop in factory output and the 63% decline in farm production between 1914 and 1920. Food requisitioning during the Civil War brought disasters besides food shortages. Cotton cultivation, for example, plummeted 95%, closing down major segments of the textile industry. The railroad network crumbled delaying the shipment of raw materials, components, and fuels, disrupting the work of factories and accelerating the economy's downward spiral. Scarce goods drove up prices until Russians found themselves living in a moneyless economy. Without money, food, or goods to barter, industrial workers lacked incentives to work—it took three Russians in 1920 to complete an industrial task performed by one in 1913.

Lenin inaugurated the New Economic Policy (NEP) in March 1921. Designed as an interim measure, the NEP restored private enterprise to the retail trade as well as to factories or workshops employing under 20 workers. It also replaced food requisitions with a definite tax that allowed peasants to sell surpluses on the free market. Also, the Soviet government stabilized the financial system and introduced a new currency while it retained control over the "commanding heights," i.e., banking, transportation, communications, major industry, wholesale commerce, and foreign trade. Once the Allied blockade was lifted, the Soviet government paid more attention to foreign trade and instituted the People's Commissariat of Foreign Trade on 22 June 1920.

Though still denied political recognition by Great Britain, the Soviets received British permission to start an Anglo-Soviet trade company. Formation of the All-Russian Cooperative Society (Arcos), Ltd., in England marked another step in the slow process of Russia's reemergence in foreign commerce. The new company sponsored a branch office in America that handled, along with a U.S. subsidiary of a British barter agency called Products Exchange (Prodexo), Soviet trade with America. Arcos and Prodexo merged in 1924 to form the Amtorg Trading Company. Incorporated in the State of New York on 27 May Amtorg conducted commercial activities, issued trade statistics, and functioned as an unofficial Soviet consulate. It also supervised a large number of small Soviet firms that opened in the U.S. in the 1920s, ranging from Amkino (films) to Platinum Products.

Soviet exports to the U.S. generally covered less than 25% of annual imports in the 1920s. Payments to and from Soviet organizations licensed for international commerce by the Foreign Trade Commissariat proceeded through the revived State Bank (Gosbank). When Arcos sold a product in the U.S., the money would be deposited locally and the dollars (generally, a ratio of five rubles for each dollar) were "sold" to Gosbank for rubles used to reimburse the Soviet exporter. The same dollars would then be "bought" from Gosbank by an importer to pay for American goods. Since the trade deficit could not be covered by rubles or U.S. loans, it required the transfer of funds in non-Soviet currencies via nations where the Soviets sold more than they bought. Soviet purchases in the U.S., then, depended on volume exports to countries other than the U.S. And like Tsarist Russia, Soviet Russia relied on the sale of agricultural products, particularly wheat and rye, as the lubricants for trade.[3]

RUSSIAN FAMINE RELIEF

Another reason for the initially low turnover in American-Soviet trade was Russia's famine that eliminated the export of its cash crops. Along with other economic misfortunes, drought threatened starvation to millions of Russians. In July 1921, author Maksim Gor'kii publicized Russia's condition with a plea for aid. The conservative U.S. Secretary of Commerce, Herbert Hoover, favorably responded to the plea in his capacity as director general of the American Relief Administration (ARA). Hoover promised food on condition that Americans then incarcerated in Soviet jails be released. Five days later, on 30 July, the Soviet government freed the first of several U.S. citizens, and Hoover quickly fulfilled his part of the bargain. The next month, Walter L. Brown, head of ARA's European Division, negotiated in Riga a relief agreement with Soviet diplomat Maksim Litvinov. Later in London, Brown signed another document temporarily lifting America's ban on Soviet gold. Over $12 million of the precious metal was absorbed as part of the relief effort enacted by Congress. President Warren G. Harding on 24 December, signed a relief bill which authorized the U.S.

Grain Corporation to expend up to $20 million for foodstuffs. When Harding issued an executive order that implemented the law via a five-member Purchasing Commission, 200 Americans had already departed for Russia as logistical support for the largely successful relief program.

American-Soviet economic activity in 1922 focused on the exchange of Soviet gold for American wheat and seed. Since the Soviet government's contribution to the relief effort amounted to only a portion of the total costs involved in acquiring, transporting, and distributing 540,000 tons of food, U.S. aid was both generous and timely in sustaining the lives of an estimated ten million Russians. Hoover and other members of the Harding Administration viewed ARA as a potential vehicle for undermining the ideological foundations of the Soviet government. And the Soviets expected the channel of communications that had been opened between the governments for humanitarian reasons to lead to a political reconciliation, including major forms of American economic and technical assistance to help in Russia's reconstruction. Neither the one nor the other occurred. Good harvests in 1922 ended the famine as well as the ARA's mission and permitted Soviet Russia to export grains in volume in 1923. The American-Soviet liquidation agreement signed on 15 June 1923 eliminated any implied or residual obligations that may have been acquired by the two governments during the relief episode. For example, the U.S. resumed its ban on Soviet gold. Thus the ARA in Soviet Russia accomplished no more and certainly no less than its most worthy public goal: it fed starving people.[4]

REVIVAL OF AMERICAN-RUSSIAN TRADE

The end to Russia's famine exposed an internal Soviet crisis in the marketing of grain, a crisis that would play a significant role in American-Soviet trade. Metropolitan Russia produced few manufactured products that could be exchanged with the countryside for food. As a result, the Soviet government gave priority to the reconstruction of the textile industry by chartering the All-Union Textile Syndicate (VTS) on 28 February 1922. Compromising 42 trusts and companies in the cotton, wool, linen, silk, and hemp industries, VTS would operate 342 factories, employ a half million workers, and control 95% of all textile production in Soviet Russia (hereafter cited as the U.S.S.R. in conformity with the 1922 constitution creating the Union of Soviet Socialist Republics). Funded by member companies and supervised by a Managing Board in Moscow, VTS served two main functions. It coordinated the manufacture and wholesale distribution of textiles. It also purchased and stored all raw materials. The need for cotton far exceeded Soviet production, and it forced the syndicate into the world market once grain exports allowed quantity imports. To ease the purchasing process, VTS opened locally incorporated export firms in Berlin, London, Riga, and Paris. Finally, in November 1923, VTS president Viktor Nogin traveled to the U.S. to open an office in New York City.

Alexander Gumberg, a well-connected Russian-American, coordinated Nogin's visit and later managed the U.S. branch of VTS, the All-Russian Textile Syndicate (ARTS). Although an American company, ARTS had a board of directors containing at least one VTS executive and, after May 1924, the chairman of Amtorg. These interlocking directorates and Moscow's holding of stock gave the U.S.S.R. strict control over Soviet companies incorporated in the United States.

TABLE 2

U.S. Trade with the U.S.S.R., 1921-1930				
(In Thousands of Dollars As % of Total)				
Year	*Exports*	*Imports*	*Total*	*U.S. Exports*
1921	15,584	1,311	16,895	0.3
1922	29,896	964	30,860	0.8
1923	7,617	1,619	9,236	0.2
1924	42,103	8,168	50,271	0.9
1925	68,906	13,120	82,026	1.4
1926	49,906	14,122	64,028	1.0
1927	64,921	12,877	77,798	1.3
1928	74,091	14,025	88,116	1.4
1929	84,011	22,551	106,562	1.6
1930	114,399	24,386	138,785	3.0

Adapted from: Department of Commerce. *Foreign Commerce and Navigation of the United States.* Washington, DC: GPO, 1922-1931.

In the fiscal year ending 30 September 1924, VTS provided member textile companies with over a half million bales of cotton. Of these bales 38,747 came from Persia (Iran), 48,350 from Egypt, 162,212 from internal sources, and 261,600 from the U.S. Although some American cotton was bought by other VTS branches especially the one in London, ARTS supplied nearly half the raw cotton processed in the U.S.S.R. and caused the dramatic jump from $9.2 million to $50.2 million in the total turnover in American-Soviet trade between 1923 and 1924. Until 1930 when the U.S.S.R. approached self-sufficiency in cotton cultivation, the fiber continued to be the single most important purchase accounting from 40% to 65% of all U.S. exports to the U.S.S.R. The balance of major Soviet activity in the U.S. export market in the 1920s fell to, tractors, automobiles and automotive parts as well as electrical and industrial machinery. For example, the Ford Motor Company sold the Soviet Union 10% of its entire tractor production for 1925. At the same time, the Soviets exported to the U.S. hides, furs, flax, bristles, sausage casings, timber products, and other, minimally processed goods including manganese (used in strengthening steel) and platinum (used in electrical connections). The advent of ARTS completed the reconstruction of American-Russian trade along lines similar in shape and amount to the exchange of goods that had occurred between the U.S. and Tsarist Russia before World War I.[5]

SOVIET DIFFERENCES WITH TSARIST RUSSIA

The surface similarities, though, should not hide the underlying differences that distinguished the Soviet Union from Tsarist Russia and the effect these differences would have on American-Soviet economic relations. As the NEP restored private enterprise to major sectors of the economy, the Soviets launched the State Planning Commission (Gosplan) in 1921. It studied resources and production figures and drafted an economic program for the entire country. At Lenin's urging, it began the first multi-year plan, in this case focusing on electrical power via the State Electrification Commission (Goelero). Goelero exceeded its goals and made available the electric power necessary for the subsequent program of general industrialization under the more familiar title, Five-Year Plan.

The NEP's highly visible free market operations in agriculture, retail sales, and small industry obscured the fact the the Soviets had fabricated the instruments for a broad-based, centrally-planned economy (CPE). In terms of international commerce, a CPE functions in a manner quite different from so-called capitalist nations. Products are not exported for profit. They are literally national sacrifices offered to the world market for cash to pay for goods identified by planners as essential to the CPE and unavailable domestically.

A CPE has potential for displaying erratic behavior in foreign commerce. And, indeed, the U.S.S.R. showed itself to be an unpredictable trading partner for the U.S. For example, the Soviet Union chose to reduce its purchases in America, causing the total turnover to fall from $82 million to $64 million between 1925 and 1926. Great Britain, Germany, Sweden, and other countries sought trade stability by negotiating commercial agreements with the Soviets as early as 1921. In contrast, the U.S. maintained its non-recognition policy and continued to the mid-1920s to be a passive trading partner which, nonetheless, secured first or second place throughout the decade as the Soviet Union's most important source of foreign goods—a tribute to economic necessity and a compliment to the quality and abundance of America's agricultural and industrial products.

Not just U.S. government restrictions, but also Soviet policy encouraged this passive behavior by preventing or restricting direct sales, investments, and other in-country activities that had attracted the interest of some U.S. businessmen in Tsarist Russia. Revolutionary Russia's economic monopoly and casual regard for foreign property ill-served the country at a time when it desperately needed assistance to restore the devastated economy. As the avowed workers' state, the Soviets antagonized the West's political and business leaders by appealing directly for help to labor in the various developed nations. One such appeal led in 1921 to the formation of the Russian-American Industrial Corporation (RAIC). It reopened and operated 15 Russian textile mills through capital and skills supplied by an American union, the Amalgamated Textile Workers. When viewed against the overall requirements of the gigantic textile industry, RAIC's small accomplishments provided more political solace than economic assistance to the Soviet regime.[6]

SOVIET USE OF CONCESSIONS

RAIC operated the mills as a concession, a major strategy introduced by the Soviets to secure outside help for the reconstruction of the Russian economy. Foreign nationals who possessed appropriate capital, administrative abilities, and/or technical skills were invited to sign a lease to rebuild a factory, reopen a mine, cut timber on a tract of land, and so forth. The first Soviet contracts bordered on the fantastic. Washington B. Vanderlip acquired a 60-year lease with exclusive coal, fishing, and oil rights on the entire Kamchatka Peninsula in northeast Siberia in October 1920. Unfortunately for the Soviets, they confused their new "Khan of Kamchatka," a California engineer, with his very distant and extremely wealthy relative, financier Frank A. Vanderlip. Later, a genuine oil magnate, Harry F. Sinclair, signed a lease to exploit petroleum reserves on the northern half of Sakhalin Island. At the time, 1922, the Japanese still occupied the area from the intervention period and would not withdraw from that portion of the island until 1925. Both contracts had also been tied, like the ones issued by Martens, to changes in the U.S. government's trade and recognition policies.

The Soviets decided in 1923 to remove some of the political baggage that had burdened so many of the concession agreements. A series of decrees issued between 8 March and 30 May implemented the policy change through the appointment of a Supreme Concessions Committee. Although it coordinated its work with such agencies as the Foreign Trade Commissariat, the committee was empowered to grant contracts without the prior approval of the Soviet of People's Commissars. By 1928 when the Five-Year Plan replaced the NEP and ended the widespread use of concessions, several hundred foreign nationals or companies had held exclusive rights in specific areas of the Soviet economy. Concessions facilitated the transfer of Western technology and shored up weak spots in the Soviet Union's material development, especially in the extractive industries. But concessions rarely influenced more than one-half of one percent of the U.S.S.R.'s total industrial output, e.g., 86 million of 14 billion rubles in 1928.

Only eight Americans held leases in the U.S.S.R. at the time such arrangements were being phased out. Of the few American concessionaires, two deserve mention. They not only illustrate U.S. participation in the NEP recovery effort, but they subsequently influenced American-Soviet relations. Railroad tycoon W. Averell Harriman received a manganese lease in the Caucasus. He later served as U.S. ambassador to the U.S.S.R. during the Second World War and functioned as a special adviser on Soviet affairs to several U.S. presidents. Armand Hammer, a medical doctor, traveled to Russia on a mission of mercy in the famine period but stayed to operate first an asbestos and then a pencil concession. He applied his experiences and profits from Russia to a number of American enterprises, eventually founding Occidental Petroleum Company. Hammer's early and favorable contacts with the Soviets thrust him into the position of a type of impressario who promoted various projects between the two countries in the 1970s and 1980s.[7]

THE REEMERGENCE OF THE AMERICAN-RUSSIAN CHAMBER OF COMMERCE

The relatively small number of Americans engaged in Soviet concessions reinforces the image of the U.S. as an inert beneficiary of Soviet initiatives to revive economic ties. Along with the NEP's private enterprise features, concessions superficially validated Western contemporary notions that the Soviets spoke communism but practiced capitalism. The government was no longer viewed as being run by blood-thirsty, bomb-throwing, bearded anarchists who delighted in destroying property. A new picture of stability emerged, one authenticated by the government's

survival under difficult circumstances and by the opening
of diplomatic and trade channels between the Soviets and
the world's principal nations. U.S. businessmen watched
their European counterparts aggressively recoup their losses
in Tsarist Russia by sales and concessions in the U.S.S.R.
Germany and Russia freely chose to renew in modified
form the commercial relations that they had shared in the
time of Tsar and Kaiser. In terms of total turnover,
Germany quickly became the U.S.S.R.'s most important
trading partner and statistically rivalled the U.S. for first
place in attracting Soviet purchases.

Soviet purchases and profits had the greatest impact on
American business attitudes, especially among recipients of
Soviet contracts. By 1925, U.S. exports to the U.S.S.R.
climbed to $68.9 million, more than double the $31.3
million in sales to Tsarist Russia in 1914. Moreover, Soviet
trade representatives received the grudging respect of U.S.
entrepreneurs. They were tenacious and meticulous in
striking a bargain and went to extremes to get the most for
their money. The Soviets compensated for their exacting,
sometimes irascible, demands by being scrupulous in
meeting their contractual obligations. After more than two
years of substantial business with the U.S.S.R., key
financiers, exporters, importers, lawyers, and industrialists
met in New York City and resurrected the moribund
American-Russian Chamber of Commerce on 11 June
1926. The impetus came from ARTS and Chase National
Bank, but key directors or firms of the old chamber found it
convenient to take a leading part in the reorganizational
move: Vice President Maurice A. Oudin of International
General Electric, Vice President Charles M. Muchnic of
American Locomotive, H. H. Westinghouse of
Westinghouse Air Brake Company, and W. H. Woodin of
American Car and Foundry Company.

The board of directors of the rejuvenated chamber
represented businesses long engaged in American-Russian
trade as well as recent participants such as concessionaire

Averell Harriman. Chase National's Reeve Schley who headed the group led the chamber toward pragmatic concerns and away from political issues. "The chamber," he stated during an early meeting, "has been revived for the sole purpose of fostering trade....It will not become a political debating society."[8] The chamber attracted at its height over 250 dues-paying members, a cross-section of corporate America ranging from American Express and Chrysler to RCA and Warner & Swasey. Companies engaged in Soviet trade gravitated toward the organization because it provided its members information. The chamber gathered and maintained in its New York offices a full library of statistics on American-Soviet commerce and on Soviet economic conditions, data the U.S. government did not have until the end of the decade.

Additionally, the chamber tried to fill the void in contacts that would have emerged during the course of political relations between two large countries. Since the U.S. failed to recognize the Soviet government, the lack of diplomatic missions also meant the absence of the full panoply of consuls and commercial agents that usually accompany the exchange of ambassadors. Thus the chamber undertook several measures to facilitate economic activities. It arranged tours of the U.S.S.R. for its members and publicized the visits to America of Soviet trade officials. The chamber also sponsored dinners and meetings to bring together American executives and Soviet representatives. Also, it soon published in the U.S.S.R. a yearbook containing a directory of members, advertisements for U.S. companies, and statistics on American industry. Finally, the chamber opened a Moscow office and employed an American who provided a number of important services: salesman plus consul, agent, and guide to U.S. executives journeying in the U.S.S.R. and wending their way through the bureaucratic maze that overlay and protected the Soviet market.

Charles H. Smith became the first chamber representative to head the Moscow office. He knew Russian and through personal encounters he understood the Soviet bureaucracy and the methods needed to complete trade transactions. His favorable connections with the Soviets, however, developed not only from his business experiences but his active participation in Communist organizations. The chamber dropped him after two years (1927-1929) because he blended this uncertain loyalty toward American capitalism with an observable lethargy that U.S. businessmen found intolerable.

In combination with the chamber's other activities, the maintenance of an independent Moscow office strained its treasury. The chamber had to rely increasingly on the generosity of Chase National Bank to subsidize its work. Although several institutions including Equitable Trust played a part in handling fund transfers and short-term credit agreements in American-Soviet trade, Chase was a major participant and beneficiary in these financial arrangements. As the chamber's debts mounted, it was left to Alexander Gumberg, formerly from ARTS, to use his Soviet contacts in 1929 to convince the Soviet Union's Chamber of Commerce for the West (reorganized in 1932 as the U.S.S.R. Chamber of Commerce) to allow the American group to share its facilities and save the expense of a separate office. The Soviet chamber operated directly under the Foreign Trade Commissariat and its chairman also held the post of Deputy Commissar of Foreign Trade. After 1929, the American-Russian Chamber of Commerce kept its office and representative in the Moscow Commodity Exchange Building, close to the Soviet personnel in charge of making foreign trade decisions.[9]

THE FIVE-YEAR PLANS

The Soviet government's willingness to assist the American chamber demonstrated the U.S.S.R.'s increased desire for U.S. goods and technology as the Soviets abandoned the NEP and entered the era of Five-Year Plans. After Lenin's death in 1924, rival claimants to his position as head of the Communist Party of the Soviet Union (CPSU) argued not whether but when and how to dismantle the NEP. Peasant confiscations in 1917 and redivisions of the land thereafter aggravated matters by chopping large and middle-sized estates into small units, increasing Russian farmsteads from an estimated 18 million in 1916 to 25.6 million in 1928. These changes in land tenure favored a shift from production for market to subsistence farming. While the NEP revived the Russian economy to its pre-war levels, it inadvertantly strengthened a peasant society that was unsupportive of the large-scale industrialization envisioned by the CPSU as necessary for the full establishment of socialism in Russia.

When the struggle over who would succeed Lenin finally ended in victory for Iosif V. Dzhugashvili (Stalin), he inaugurated the Five-Year Plan and the collectivization of agriculture in 1928-29. The two movements were inextricably linked, for the one helped pay for the other. Within a few years the Soviet government forcibly merged 25.6 million individual farms into 250,000 collectives. This new revolution was far more sweeping in results and costly in human life and misery than the political upheavals of 1917. Five million farm families (approximately 24 million people) disappeared from rural Russia—one-half went to towns and cities, one-half either perished or went to labor camps for refusing to give up their land. The Soviet government came to exert, perhaps for the first time, genuine authority in the countryside through its absolute mastery over peasant labor and control of agricultural production. It paid collectives only a fraction of the prices charged consumers for food. Along with artificially low industrial wages, rationing, and sales taxes on consumer items, this "tax" on collectives served to finance the Soviet Union's Five-Year Plan.

Collectivized agriculture proved to be a perennial weakness in the Soviet economy, but it did generate investment for the remarkable program of industrialization. Soviet planners certainly made errors and wasted resources; nevertheless, industrial growth rose tremendously at annual rates of 12 to 14 percent and moved the U.S.S.R. from fifth to second place among industrialized nations, an impressive feat accomplished in the midst of a world-wide economic depression. The Soviets exaggerated their successes claiming that goals in the first plan had been reached by 31 December 1932. The Second Five-Year Plan (1933-1937) was followed by a Third (1938-1942), which was interrupted by the German invasion of June 1941. While the plans exhibited distinctive goals, they all stressed the capital construction and capital production (goods to make other goods) associated with heavy industry.

The First Five-Year Plan would not have achieved its aims without key imports and technical assistance from the West and in particular from the United States. This was illustrated by the 36% increase in Soviet purchases in America that caused the total trade to rise from $88.1 million in 1928 to $138.8 million in 1930. America supplied 25% of all Soviet imports followed by Germany (23.7%) and then Great Britain (7.6%).

A major aim of the First Five Year Plan was to create a large Soviet automobile industry. The Ford Motor Company agreed to supply the Soviets with technical assistance in constructing a plant at Nizhnii-Novgorod (Gor'kii), one designed to manufacture 100,000 units per year. The Ford contract, including its built-in technical aid features, typified the Soviet practice of gaining Western know-how and assistance without resorting to concession agreements.

TABLE 3

Impact of Five-Year Plan on Soviet Purchases in U.S.		
(Percentage Distribution by Value)		
American Products	*1927*	*1931*
Cacao Beans	0.4	—
Leather or LeatherProducts	3.3	—
White Resin	0.7	—
Rubber or Rubber Products	2.8	—
Tanning Products	0.9	—
Sheep wool	1.1	—
Cotton	50.1	—
Ferrous Metals	0.7	0.6
Nonferrous Metals	9.9	1.2
Metallic Products	2.8	2.3
Machinery and Parts	8.5	33.5
Agricultural Machinery and Parts	2.1	8.4
Electrical Machinery and Parts	2.2	5.6
Tractors and Parts	5.3	34.3
Automotive Equipment	1.6	10.7
Unclassified	7.6	3.4
	100.0	100.0

Adapted from Mikhail V. Condoide, *Russian-American Trade: A Study of the Foreign Trade Monopoly*. Columbus: The Ohio State University, 1946.

One aspect of the Ford deal illustrates another characteristic of Soviet commercial arrangements in the early stages of the First Five-Year Plan. The latter enabled the Foreign Trade Commissariat and the import groups it licensed to project needs over a period of several years. Through its American agent, Amtorg Trading Company, Inc., the Soviet government negotiated over 200 extended contracts with American firms. The benefits for U.S.

exporters in terms of production planning and resource allocation were considerable.   In return, the Soviets frequently insisted on credits that permitted the U.S.S.R. to receive early delivery of American goods and settle accounts at a later date.   The U.S. State Department continued to prohibit loans and bonds to finance Soviet trade and development.   However, in October 1928, International General Electric (IGE) offered the Soviets long-term credits in its five-year, $25 million sales contract for electrical equipment.   Volume business with the U.S.S.R. then did prompt a slight shift in the position of the U.S. government.   In fact, by 1929 the U.S. Department of Commerce, sensitive to the needs and interests of American business, issued monthly bulletins on Soviet trade and economic conditions.

The Soviet Union's conduct in the American export market gained a moderately favorable response from the U.S. government and resulted in the acquisition of key manufactures designed to contribute maximum benefits to the U.S.S.R.'s material progress.   Equally important to this progress were technical aid contracts, ones not tied to U.S. sales.   The Soviets bought from the West technical processes and trade secrets as well as the services of technicians and engineers and employed these technologies and personnel in building and modernizing Russia's industrial plant.   By 1931, the U.S.S.R. had negotiated 134 technical aid agreements, the bulk of which went to American and German firms.   Several of the more important contracts with U.S. companies were: Austin Company prepared the architectural designs for over 600 Soviet plants; Albert Kahn Company secured the contract for the Stalingrad Tractor Factory; Stuart, James & Cooke revamped the U.S.S.R.'s coal industry; Freyn Engineering directed the construction of the steel mill at Kuznetsk; and Arthur G. McKee and Company planned the U.S.S.R.'s most famous steel mill at Magnitogorsk.   At the dawn of the 1930s over 1,000 U.S. engineers worked in the U.S.S.R.

prompting the exaggerated aphorism that the Soviets conceived the First Five-Year Plan, but Americans literally engineered it. During the 1920s, many U.S. businessmen moved from passive witnesses to active participants in American-Soviet economic relations.[10]

NOTES

1. Quote from *New York Times*, 20 March 1917.

2. Ibid., 19 August 1920. See also: George F. Kennan, *Soviet-American Relations, 1917-1920*, 2 vols. (New York: Atheneum, 1967); James K. Libbey, "The American-Russian Chamber of Commerce," *Diplomatic History* 9 (Summer 1985), 233-248; Robert D. Warth, *The Allies and the Russian Revolution: From the Fall of the Monarchy to the Peace of Brest-Litovsk* (Durham: Duke University Press, 1954).

3. James K. Libbey, *Alexander Gumberg and Soviet-American Relations, 1917-1933* (Lexington: University Press of Kentucky, 1977), 128. See also Edward Hallett Carr, *The Bolshevik Revolution*, Vol. 2 (New York: Macmillan, 1952); Leonid B. Krassin, *Voprosy vneshnei torgovli* (Moscow: Gosizdat, 1928); Joan Hoff Wilson, *Ideology and Economics: U.S. Relations with the Soviet Union, 1918-1933* (Columbia: University of Missouri Press, 1974).

4. Benjamin M. Weissman, *Herbert Hoover and Russian Famine Relief to Soviet Russia, 1921-23* (Stanford: Hoover Institution, 1974), 175-178. See also Harold H. Fisher, *The Famine in Soviet Russia, 1919-1923: The Operations of the American Relief Administration* (New York: Macmillan, 1927); Benjamin M. Weissman, "Herbert Hoover's 'Treaty' with Soviet Russia: August 20, 1921," *Slavic Review* 28 (June 1969), 276-288.

5. Philip S. Gillette, "Conditions of American-Soviet Commerce: The Beginning of Direct Cotton Trade, 1923-1924," *Soviet Union* 1 (1974), 74-93; James K. Libbey, "Nogin, Viktor Pavlovich (1878-1924)," in Joseph L. Wieczynski, ed., *The Modern Encyclopedia of Russian and Soviet History*, Vol. 25 (Gulf Breeze: Academic International, 1981), 43-45; "Russia's Cotton Come-Back," *Commerce and Finance*, No. 40 (October 7, 1925), 1977.

6. Mikhail V. Condoide, *Russian-American Trade: A Study of the Foreign-Trade Monopoly* (Columbus: Ohio State University Press, 1946), 40; *Economic Handbook of the Soviet Union* (New York: American-Russian Chamber of Commerce, 1931), 105. See also

Glen Alden Smith, *Soviet Foreign Trade: Organization, Operations, and Policy, 1918-1971* (New York: Praeger, 1973).

7. Pauline Tompkins, *American-Russian Relations in the Far East* (New York: Macmillan, 1949), 185-187; Joan Hoff Wilson, "The Role of the Business Community in American Relations with Russia and Europe, 1920-1933." Ph.D. Diss., University of California, 1966, 309-310. See also Antony C. Sutton, *Western Technology and Soviet Economic Development 1917 to 1930* (Stanford: Hoover Institution, 1968).

8. Quote from printed brochure, 23 July 1926, American-Russian Chamber of Commerce Papers, State Historical Society of Wisconsin, Box 21.

9. Libbey, "The American-Russian Chamber of Commerce," 239-241; James K. Libbey, "Chamber of Commerce for the West," in Joseph L. Wieczynski, ed., *The Modern Encyclopedia of Russian and Soviet History*, Vol. 6 (Gulf Breeze: Academic International, 1978), 197-199. See also *Handbook of the Soviet Union* (New York: American-Russian Chamber of Commerce, 1936).

10. Lewis S. Feur, "Travelers to the Soviet Union, 1917-1932: The Formation of a Component of New Deal Ideology," *American Quarterly* 14 (Summer 1962), 119-149; John P. McKay, "Foreign Enterprise in Russian and Soviet Industry: A Long-term Perspective," *Business History Review* 48 (Autumn 1974), 336-356. See also James K. Libbey, "Soviet-American Trade," in Joseph L. Wieczynski, ed., *The Modern Encyclopedia of Russian and Soviet History*, Vol. 36 (Gulf Breeze: Academic International, 1984), 195-202. See also Dmitrii D. Mishutin, *Vneshniaia torgovlia i industrializatsiia SSSR* (Moscow: Mezhdunarodnaia kniga, 1938).

Chapter 3

ECONOMIC WEAPONS IN PEACE AND WAR

In October 1929, the value of stocks quoted on the New York Exchange fell 37%, heralding the start of the Great Depression. The best efforts of financiers could not stem the collapse as the U.S. credit structure imploded under speculative and worthless paper. Banks failed; factories closed; prices dropped; personal income fell by 50%; and unemployment rose from five million in 1930 to 14 million in 1932, leaving one-third of the labor force out of work. The U.S. panic triggered an international financial crisis that eventually led to a 38% slowdown in production world-wide. And U.S. policy aggravated matters when Congress approved and President Herbert Hoover signed into law the Hawley-Smoot Tariff in June 1930. It raised import duties to an all-time high and amply fulfilled the worst fears of its critics. The protectionist measure sparked a retaliatory tariff war, raising global barriers to international commerce. In the space of three years, the total turnover in America's foreign trade plummeted 70%, from $9.6 billion in 1929 to $2.9 billion in 1932.

THE EFFECT OF THE GREAT DEPRESSION

By contrast, the Soviet Union's internal growth and development continued at a remarkable pace, one that seemed impervious to the economic horrors endured by the U.S. and other industrialized nations. The Depression initially had no noticeable effect on American-Soviet trade. American sales to the Soviets actually increased in dollar amounts from $84.0 million in 1929 to $114.4 million in 1930 before decreasing slightly in 1931 to $103.7 million. Considering the drop in America's overseas commerce, the Soviet Union's relative position as a market for U.S. goods had jumped threefold to make the U.S.S.R. the one bright spot in the otherwise dark picture presented by America's export business. Long-term commitments, rather than new orders, partly explain the continuation of volume sales to the U.S.S.R. As purchasing power fell and import duties rose in Europe, the U.S.S.R. found it more difficult to sell adequate amounts of goods to buy the imports identified as crucial for the Five-Year Plan. The problem was magnified by trade with America where Soviet exports generally paid for less than 25% of imports. In the 1920s, the U.S.S.R. occasionally transferred funds from European sales to redress the balance in American-Soviet commerce, but with the Depression such discretionary capital disappeared.

Financing became a prerequisite if the Soviets hoped to continue the flow of Western products into the U.S.S.R. Moscow possessed an excellent record in business affairs, and it cashed in on its sound reputation by negotiating government-guaranteed loans or export credits with Germany, Italy, Great Britain, Norway, Denmark, Japan, Austria, Poland, Finland, Czechoslovakia, and Latvia. These arrangements allowed the Soviets to take immediate delivery of goods on payments ranging from 30% to 40% with the balance due over a specified period of time. Belatedly, the U.S. altered its policies enough to permit the Soviets to market in America two long-term, gold-backed bond issues worth a total of $11 million in 1932 and 1933.

And in July of 1933, the U.S. government, through its Reconstruction Finance Corporation, advanced a $4 million line of credit to Amtorg to help finance the sale of U.S. cotton to the Soviet Union.

By then, however, a transformation had occurred in the Soviet Union's pattern of commerce, one with catastrophic results for America's export trade with the the U.S.S.R. Sales plunged 88% between 1931 and 1932, and the next year the U.S.S.R. only bought $8.9 million worth of American products. Countries that furnished guaranteed loans or credits enjoyed trade increases with the Soviets, but the U.S. share of the Russian market decreased from 25% in 1930 to 4.5% in 1932. Italy's share, for example, rose from 1.0% to 3.9% and Great Britain's nearly doubled from 7.6% to 13.1%. Germany was the main beneficiary shipping 46.5% of all goods entering the Soviet Union in 1932, a figure reminiscent of the Tsarist era. The U.S.'s failure in the early Depression years to finance Soviet trade is only a partial explanation why the Soviets withdrew their business from America. After all, from the late 1920s the U.S. government no longer interfered with American companies offering in-house financing to the Soviets. The other part of the explanation is that the U.S.S.R. used economics to punish American behavior and achieve political goals.

The pivotal event occurred on 1 July 1930, when U.S. Customs temporarily held up cargos of Russian pulpwood under authority of the recently enacted Hawley-Smoot Tariff. Section 307 allowed the U.S. to embargo goods produced by convict labor. U.S. Treasury Secretary, Andrew Mellon, had criticized the Soviet practice of unloading cheap matches on the depressed American economy. Mellon's position was peculiar for at the time he personally provided them with several million dollars through purchases of Soviet art treasures.

TABLE 4

U.S.Trade with the U.S.S.R., 1931-1941				
(In Thousands of Dollars As%ofTotal)				
Year	*Exports*	*Imports*	*Total U.S. Exports*	
1931	103,717	13,206	116,923	4.3
1932	12,641	9,736	22,377	0.8
1933	8,997	12,114	21,111	0.5
1934	15,011	12,337	27,348	0.7
1935	24,743	17,809	42,552	1.1
1936	33,427	20,517	53,944	1.4
1937	42,892	30,763	73,655	1.3
1938	69,691	24,034	93,725	2.3
1939	56,638	25,023	81,661	1.8
1940	86,943	22,274	109,217	2.2
1941	108,122	30,036	138,158	2.1

Adapted from: U.S. Department of Commerce, *Foreign Commerce and Navigation of the United States.* Washington, DC: GPO, Annual.

On July 25, Assistant Secretary of the Treasury Seymour Lowman banned all Soviet pulpwood, and officials hinted that most other Soviet products including matches would be forbidden. Dumping, not human, rights was the issue that concerned some U.S. political figures whose views were shaped not by facts but by their anti-Communist ideology. They assumed the Soviets used dumping to cause further damage to the country's already weakened economic condition. Most Soviet exports, however, such as manganese, caviar, and platinum did not compete with American goods or did not measure more than a fraction of one percent of American output. Mellon's attack on Soviet matches was unenlightened as Russian matches vied with products of an international cartel headquartered in Sweden. The Soviets, whose foreign trade concerns focused on exports as a necessary evil to acquire vital imports, did indeed sell goods below costs. But, in the case of matches, the Soviets competed with a cartel that also dumped its product in the United States.

Directors of the American-Russian Chamber who had a better grasp of the facts contacted Mellon, President Hoover, and Robert P. Lamont, Secretary of Commerce. After a brief investigation, the infamous pulpwood was unloaded in U.S. ports. Although President Hoover opposed an embargo of Soviet goods, the Treasury Department retained the right, until 1934, to challenge any ship carrying Soviet products and left it to importers to prove convict labor had not been used. The resulting uncertainty wreaked havoc with American-Soviet conmerce because the Soviets used trade acceptances and warehouse receipts on its exports to the U.S. to initiate financing for its purchases of American goods. Without financing and without guarantees that its products would be received in the U.S., the U.S.S.R. could ill afford to place new, large-scale orders in America.

Moreover, the Soviets chose to use less, not more trade to do mischief in the American economy and to achieve political change. On 20 October 1930, the Soviet government issued a decree authorizing the People's Commissariat of Foreign Trade to take steps against those nations that hindered the normal importation of Soviet goods. The decree empowered the Commissariat to reduce or eliminate its purchases in offending countries. The new measure bolstered a law of 17 March 1927, permitting the Commissariat to use foreign trade to discriminate against countries withholding diplomatic recognition from the U.S.S.R. Moscow wanted Washington to eliminate its trade restrictions and acknowledge the legitimate existence of the Soviet regime. In September 1931, the CPSU's governing Politburo heard a report from Deputy Commissar of Foreign Affairs Nikolai N. Krestinskii that suggested: "The loss of Soviet markets, the significance of which for some areas of American industry is tremendous in the period of [economic] crisis, will be an incentive to American business and political circles to review their traditional position of nonrecognition of the U.S.S.R."[1]

RECOGNITION AND RUSSIAN INDEBTEDNESS

The sharp decline in Soviet trade did alter the views and attitudes of some political and business leaders. Disastrous trade figures for 1932 prompted the American-Russian Chamber of Commerce to abandon its frequently stated position of avoiding political questions. On 13 July 1933, the chamber issued a press release urging "early recognition, to be followed by the negotiation of an equitable trade agreement."[2] The Roosevelt administration permitted the Soviets to float a bond issue in the U.S. and authorized a governmental loan to a Soviet company. It also wanted to revive Soviet trade as a modest step in promoting U.S. economic recovery. Many reasons other than economic account for the establishment of diplomatic relations between the U.S. and U.S.S.R. in November 1933. Among the more important ones must be counted the desire of both governments for recognition to symbolize to the world a merger of foreign policy interests, i.e., American-Soviet cooperation to check the expansionist designs of Germany and Japan in Europe and Asia.

The exchange of ambassadors, William Bullitt to Moscow and Aleksandr Troianovskii to Washington, failed to fulfill the economic and political aspirations raised by the recognition agreements concluded on 17 November. Leaders in both countries understood the benefits for peace that American-Soviet collaboration might bring; yet they were unable or unwilling to overcome the list of negatives that prevented closer ties: ideological differences, Russian xenophobia, American isolationism, bureaucratic inertia, simple ignorance, plus a 16-year political history characterized by bitter animosity and mutual distrust. Also,

Russian indebtedness to the U.S. became an early problem that obstructed cooperation in economic and political affairs. The Treasury Department added up all the debts Russia owed to the citizens and government of the U.S., a total exceeding $636 million. On the other hand, the Soviets held counterclaims based largely on America's military intervention in North Russia and Siberia during the Russian Civil War.

Both sides offered compromises; however, of the three U.S. preconditions to diplomatic relations (debt settlement, religious rights, Communist propaganda), the subject of debts led to the most acrimonious and protracted discussion. The Roosevelt administration focused on public debts, or more precisely, the $187.7 million in U.S. funds spent by the Provisional Government in fighting Germany in 1917. Similarly, the Soviets adjusted their counterclaims by limiting them to American damages in North Russia. U.S. government documents apparently convinced Foreign Affairs Commissar Maksim Litvinov that American troops went to Siberia primarily to safeguard Russia's territorial integrity from military encroachment by Japan. Despite these accommodations, American-Soviet talks could only reach a broad understanding that the Soviet obligation would be between $75 million and $150 million and that payment could take the form of extra interest on a U.S. loan or credit which the Soviets would use to buy American articles. Other problems such as interest on the debt were virtually ignored.

Following the establishment of diplomatic ties, talks on the debt issue moved to Moscow where Ambassador William Bullitt and Litvinov found their positions too far apart to arrive at a satisfactory conclusion. Negotiations continued off and on in both capitals for the next seven years but the problem remained immune to solution. The inconclusive debt talks also dimmed prospects for a major and direct U.S. loan to the U.S.S.R. to promote trade.

President Roosevelt issued an Executive Order in February 1934 that created the Export-Import Bank, an institution initially funded with $11 million and primarily designed to finance American-Soviet commerce. Charles E. Stuart became executive vice president of the new bank. Stuart belonged to the Board of Directors of the American-Russian Chamber of Commerce and presided over the firm of Stuart, James & Cooke which had held a technical assistance contract from the Soviet government. The bank adopted a resolution that prohibited the extension of credits to nations in default of governmental loans. It did finance U.S. exporters, regardless of the destination of their products, but the Soviets found such restricted loans of limited value. Other unfavorable news appeared in April 1934 with the passage of the Johnson Act. Similar to the bank's proviso, it stated that no person or private corporation under American jurisdiction could lend money to a government that had not paid its debts to the United States.[3]

THE SOVIETS AND SELF-SUFFICIENCY

The opening of embassies in Moscow and Washington did little to advance American-Soviet economic interests. For example, the 1934 trade turnover totaled $27.3 million, far below the levels achieved shortly before the establishment of formal links between the two countries. And U.S. sales to the Soviet Union were only $15 million or slightly less than the dollar amounts of U.S. exports to Soviet Russia in 1921. The Second Five-Year Plan stressed the development of heavy industry but without relying on imports and personnel from the West. The Soviets sought self-sufficiency as a means of preserving the U.S.S.R. against its real and imagined capitalist enemies that threatened the state. When the expected revolutions in the West did not materialize (except briefly in Hungary), internationalists such as Lev Trotskii fell from grace in the

CPSU to be replaced by the ideologically conservative Stalin who spoke of building "socialism in one country."

Japan's military operations in China and the rise to power of Hitler in Germany gave renewed purpose to the Soviet drive toward self-sufficiency. Externally, the Soviets sought a rapprochement with the Western democracies, signed nonaggression pacts with several countries, and joined the League of Nations in 1934. National Communist parties were instructed to cooperate, in their respective countries, with other political groups interested in checking Fascist aggression. Internally, the insecurity raised by the appearance of hostile, anti-Communist military powers at both ends of the U.S.S.R. elicited an xenophobia of unparalleled dimensions. By 1933 most of the estimated 6,800 foreign technicians and engineers who had been hired by the Soviets during the First Five-Year Plan were gone. By using discriminatory currency exchange and closing special retail stores for foreigners, the Soviet government did everything to discourage the presence of all but a handful of carefully selected, closely watched Western specialists whose presence was deemed vital to the economic improvement, i.e., national security, of the Soviet Union.

The fear of foreigners and the quest for economic independence prompted a reorganization of the Foreign Trade Commissariat and caused changes in the overall pattern of the Soviet Union's international commerce. Soviet imports fell from 4.83 billion rubles in 1931 to 1.01 billion rubles in 1934. This reduction in imports enabled the Soviets to finance their trade with cash or gold instead of renewing or expanding their large-scale credit arrangements with various industrialized nations. From 1933 through 1937 exports exceeded the value of imports and resulted in a build-up of foreign exchange that the Soviets applied toward current purchases and old debts. By 1935 the debt dropped below $100 million U.S. dollars, and three years later the Soviets had repaid virtually all their commercial obligations.   Meanwhile, the U.S.S.R. streamlined and centralized its foreign trade monopoly.   It forced trading groups into export or import monopoly combines, commonly referred to as foreign trade organizations (FTOs).   The FTOs specialized in specific products (chemicals, grains, etc.) and gained the right on 27 July 1935, to sign trade transactions.   FTOs conducted their business in Moscow under the close supervision of the Foreign Trade Commissariat and by 1936 almost every foreign trade deal was completed in Moscow rather than through Soviet trade delegations located in each major nation.   Amtorg, for example, admitted to U.S. businessmen as early as 1935 that it could no longer initiate or approve contracts and would function only as an inspector of American goods shipped to Russia.

Such exacting requirements in foreign trade illustrate a unique characteristic of the Soviet Union's material progress.   Unlike other developing countries, the U.S.S.R. reaped the benefits of foreign investment without surrendering any political or economic control to American or Western capitalists.   The Soviets accomplished this feat by literally buying the West's machines, technologies, and experts and applying these external resources to internal improvements through the use of Soviet capital, labor, land, and entrepreneurial talents.   Thus the profits from Western technology accrued to the Soviet economy, not to foreign investors.   This is to temper, not diminish, the significance of the interaction between western technology and Soviet industrialization, an interaction that continued at a less observable level after the Soviets reduced their use of products and personnel from the West.

A Soviet factory built by Austin Company in 1930 might remain in operation for years and its design features copied to reemerge in dozens of buildings for decades to come.   The Soviet contract with International General Electric in 1928 transferred the latest electrical welding technology that percolated in the 1930s through a host of

Soviet industries. These two examples would have to be multiplied a thousand times before an adequate picture could be painted of the continuing impact of the West on Soviet development. And the human factor should not be ignored. Thousands of Soviet engineers, technicians, and skilled laborers worked alongside their foreign counterparts during the First Five-Year Plan and applied their knowledge to the tasks outlined in the Second and Third Plans. Other Soviets traveled abroad. In the single 18-month period from 1 January 1929 to 15 June 1930, 842 Russians visited America to train with U.S. industrial specialists as part of the numerous American-Soviet technical aid agreements.

If not for the deteriorating international situation, the initial burst of Western training and technology of the First Five-Year Plan might have made the Soviet achievement of economic independence more real than apparent. In November 1936, Germany and Japan fulfilled the U.S.S.R.'s worst nightmare by concluding the Anti-Comintern Pact aimed specifically at the Soviet Union. Worst of all from the Soviet view, such powers as France, Great Britain, and the U.S. hesitated, compromised, stressed nonintervention, or employed only gestures rather than taking actual measures to challenge Fascism. Under these circumstances, the Soviets tried to modernize and equip their armed forces. In the midst of the Second Five-Year Plan, the Soviet government postponed the proposed expansion of consumer goods to redirect resources to armaments. Tanks replaced tractors or gun carriers replaced automobiles in the production of existing factories. Military requirements also influenced foreign trade as imports rebounded 42% between 1934 and 1938. This time, however, the U.S.S.R. was less interested in capital equipment than in highly sophisticated, military-oriented technology.[4]

AMERICAN-SOVIET TRADE AGREEMENTS

Only a few nations—primarily Germany and the U.S. possessed the facilities and skills required to design and produce the advanced military hardware that the Soviets wanted. But since 30 January 1933, when Hitler assumed the post of chancellor, the bottom had fallen out of German-Soviet economic and political relations. Germany's anti-Communist rhetoric and policies persuaded the U.S.S.R. to look to America as a major source of goods and technologies that would bolster her national security. America's share of Soviet imports climbed to 28.5% while Germany's fell to 4.7% by 1938. The same year, the Soviets bought nearly $70 million worth of U.S. articles, a figure comparable in dollar amounts to the level of Soviet purchases in the American market in the late 1920s.

One tool used to smooth the path for this revival was the American-Soviet Trade Agreement of 1935. Signed by Ambassador Bullitt and Foreign Affairs Commissar Litvinov in Moscow on 13 July, it reflected a commitment by both parties not to permit the troublesome debt negotiations to rupture relations. Under the accord, the U.S.S.R. promised to buy in 12 months' time at least $30 million in American goods in return for most-favored-nation tariff treatment by the U.S. government. America thus extended to the U.S.S.R. the lower (50% in some cases) tariff rates already granted to Belgium, Haiti, and Sweden under the Reciprocal Trade Agreements Act. The foreign trade monopoly prevented the U.S.S.R. from offering tariff concessions, the chief element in the U.S. law that gave the Roosevelt administration a way to ease, on a nation-by-nation basis, the debilitating effects of the Hawley-Smoot Act. U.S. firms did not compete with the companies of other nations in selling their products on an open market within the U.S.S.R.; goods entered the country without prejudicial or preferential treatment because the Soviet government bought them. And the notion of import duties as a protective device against foreign competition was alien to the Soviet Union's centrally-planned economy. Regardless, the inability to reciprocate in tariff concessions prompted Bullitt and Litvinov to compensate with the Soviet pledge on purchasing amounts.

The two governments annually extended or renegotiated the American-Soviet Trade Agreement until 1942 when the Americans and Russians renewed this commercial accord for an indefinite period. It remained in effect until the U.S. Congress required the President to terminate the compact in the Trade Agreements Extension Act of 1951. (Section 5 of the new 1951 act prohibited the government from continuing its most-favored-nation tariff treatment with the Soviet Union.) The Soviets took advantage of the favorable duties by increasing the value of their exports to America from $12.3 million in 1934 to $30.7 million in 1937. With the balance of trade at a more equitable level, the Soviets set about procuring those products and technologies that would buttress Soviet military capabilities. The types of Soviet goods sold in the U.S. remained essentially the same as those shipped to America in the late 1920s, but imports differed significantly from those articles bought during the First Five-Year Plan. Instead of tractors, automobiles, and basic machine tools such as lathes, the U.S.S.R. secured or tried to secure American aircraft, petroleum processes, and modern warships.

Russia's indigenous aircraft industry had suffered an enormous setback after the Revolution because prominent aeronautical engineers fled the country. The Soviets partially countered this loss in the 1920s with covert arrangements with the German military and manufacturers, such as Junkers, to build planes and operate flying schools on Soviet soil in violation of the Versailles Treaty. The links with Germany snapped, of course, after 1932. Thus between 1934 and 1939, the Soviets moved to the American market and bought a small number of airplanes from a large number of firms including Consolidated, Douglas, Martin, Republic, Seversky, Sikorsky, and Vultee.

They hoped to assimilate the technological improvements found in these aircraft and adapt them to their own models. A rare technical assistance agreement was concluded with Douglas Aircraft Company on 15 July 1936. Douglas sold a complete set of plans that enabled the Soviet Union to duplicate the famous twin-engined transport, the DC-3. And in 1937 the Soviets invited engineers from Vultee Aircraft, developers of the V-11 attack bomber, to spend six months in Moscow to assist them in opening a new factory near the capital city. At the same time, American machine tools were used to update the aircraft industry. The Soviets bought hydraulic presses to stamp aircraft panels from Birdsboro Steel Foundry & Machine Company and Lake Erie Engineering Corporation. Finally, from 1936 to 1938, the U.S.S.R. awarded contracts to several U.S. firms such as Universal Oil, Petroleum Engineering, and Lummus Company to help the Soviets expand their refining capacity at Baku and create new refineries near Ufa. One objective in this expansion was to produce high octane aviation fuels based on American-supplied processes.

The relative success enjoyed by the U.S.S.R. in accumulating U.S. aircraft and related technologies is in sharp contrast to its failure to obtain American warships. As early as November 1936, Soviet representatives began exploring with the U.S. State Department the possibility of buying a battleship, and they set up the Carp Corporation to conduct negotiations and handle arrangements. The contemporary Soviet fleet consisted mainly of refitted ships from the Tsarist era, and the U.S.S.R. lacked the facilities and equipment to construct heavily armed ships. Not only did the State Department give its approval, but President Roosevelt personally endorsed the sale. In a time when American foreign policy tended to be erratic and hence ineffective, the U.S. government's most consistent strategy focused on gestures of cooperation with the Soviet Union as a vague warning to the revisionist nations of Germany and Japan.

One such gesture was FDR's reception for the Russian aviators who flew across the North Pole, landing at Vancouver, Washington on 23 June 1937. Another found a U.S. naval squadron under Admiral Harry E. Yarnell making a friendly visit to the Soviet port of Vladivostok in July 1937. Yet another was the well-publicized deal to sell the Soviets a battleship. Despite FDR's support, the Soviet order went unfulfilled. In disobedience to its Commander-in-Chief, the Navy Department employed every tactic, other than outright refusal, to delay indefinitely the Soviet acquisition of an American battleship.   The Navy procrastinated in releasing approvals for classified equipment and quietly cautioned shipbuilders that if they accepted a Russian contract they might lose the Navy's business. By 1939, the shipyards did not have the space to work on a Russian order because of the U.S. rearmament program. Later that same year, the Molotov-Ribbentrop agreements clouded American-Soviet relations, effectively ending the matter.[5]

THE NAZI-SOVIET PACT

From the Soviet position, the lack of genuine cooperation with the U.S. and other democratic powers left the U.S.S.R. in an isolated, vulnerable position. Japan provoked incidents leading to corps-sized battles between Japanese and Soviet troops along the Manchurian and Mongolian borders in 1938 and 1939. Meanwhile, Hitler pressed his publicly stated plans of expansion by seizing Austria in March 1938. Now, Soviet leaders pondered Hitler's other promises: to destroy communism and acquire living space for the German people at the expense of Russia and the Slavs in Eastern Europe. The Soviet Union's carefully constructed edifice of collective security collapsed in September 1938 at Munich where Britain and France, without consulting the Soviets, capitulated to Hitler's demand for Czechoslovakia's Sudetenland.   Western unpreparedness and unwillingness to fight Hitler filtered into Soviet minds as collusion.

In May 1939, Stalin removed Litvinov, who had been closely identified with collective security, and replaced him in the Foreign Affairs Commissariat with Viacheslav M. Molotov. Molotov looked for a way to deflect hostilities from Soviet borders and accomplished the goal by secret negotiations that resulted in the German-Soviet Nonaggression Treaty of 23 August 1939. From Moscow's vantage point, it was a stunning diplomatic victory. Germany attacked Poland on 1 September and two days later France and Great Britain declared war on the Third Reich; yet the Soviet Union remained at peace. The Soviets garnered two additional dividends: in a secret protocol, they received a free hand in dealing with Russian territories lost in World War I from Finland to Bessarabia. The Molotov-Ribbentrop agreement also surprised and disheartened Germany's Anti-Comintern partner, Japan. Almost immediately, Japanese troops reduced their pressure on the Soviet Far East, and, on 15 September, there was a Japanese-Soviet pledge to negotiate all border disputes. The Nazi-Soviet Pact did not shock official Washington because diplomatic intelligence had forewarned the Roosevelt administration of the direction of the discussions between Berlin and Moscow. Thereafter, the U.S. adopted a cautious policy toward the U.S.S.R., hoping to undermine the Hitler-Stalin alliance and prevent a similar pact from being formed between Tokyo and Moscow.

In December 1939, the Soviets had demanded territory from Finland in order to expand the defensive perimeter around Leningrad (Petrograd, until 1924). When the Finns refused, the U.S.S.R. conducted an initially unsuccessful invasion. As a small democracy, Finland gained the sympathy of the American people, a compassion strengthened by ethnic ties in some cases and the knowledge that it had been the only European country to maintain regular payments on its World War I debts. After

Soviet planes bombed Finnish cities in December, President Roosevelt expressed America's outrage and called for a "moral embargo" against the Soviet Union. It was designed to punish the U.S.S.R. by ending shipments of U.S. planes, aircraft parts, and aviation fuels.

While American contempt for Soviet actions in Finland led to the temporary moral embargo, the same sentiment permanently destroyed the American-Russian Chamber of Commerce. Premonitions of its demise occurred shortly after the Nazi-Soviet Pact. Moscow representative Spencer Williams confided to Reeve Schley that the newly found friendship between Moscow and Berlin left "no promising field for the Chamber now unless there is a sudden, radical shift in the Soviet orientation again."[6] Combined with the Soviet Union's Winter War with Finland, the prospect of Russians acting as middlemen for Nazi Germany's war industry prompted most American businessmen to end their financial support of the chamber. By January 1940, it ceased to exist except on paper. More than three decades would pass before a similar institution emerged to promote the commerce shared by the two countries.

Nevertheless, American-Soviet trade jumped from $81.6 million in 1939 to $109.2 million in 1940, an expansion due primarily to $30 million in purchases that offset a slight decline in Soviet exports. Two details distinguished American-Soviet trade: first, U.S. businessmen demonstrated a passivity that had characterized their behavior toward Soviet commercial activity during the first half of the 1920s. Second, the moral embargo forced the Soviets to move away from aviation products. Major substitutions included refined copper and brass plates, articles accounting for 23% of all U.S.S.R. purchases in 1940. The metal and alloy were of military significance for use in ammunition. On the surface these expenditures seemed curious because Soviet lands yield huge deposits of zinc and copper; however, geography and the British navy encouraged Germany to use its new "friend" as a conduit for its acquisition of strategic materials.

Moscow's commerce with Berlin, infamous victory over Finland, and subsequent reoccupation of the Baltic states did not deflect the Roosevelt administration from its basic position. Germany's rapid conquests of Denmark, Norway, the Low Countries, and France in the spring of 1940 justified the U.S.'s belief that Hitler posed a greater menace than Stalin. Then too, Hitler's well-received overtures to Finland and interest in the Balkans gave the U.S.S.R. reasons to worry. As early as July 1940, Under Secretary of State Sumner Welles and Soviet Ambassador Konstantin Umanskii began exploring common areas of concern. Other than keeping the door open for future options, the on-going talks bore few tangible results. The Soviets wished to avoid jeopardizing the Nazi-Soviet Pact; while the U.S. refused to recognize the U.S.S.R.'s reannexation of Estonia, Latvia, and Lithuania. Nevertheless, the talks led to an understanding on Soviet relations with Japan and the removal of the American embargo on 21 January 1941.[7]

LEND-LEASE

As an indirect consequence of these talks FDR warded off legislative attempts to exclude the Soviet Union from the Lend-Lease Act passed by Congress on 10 March 1941. Thus Lend-Lease, originally America's financial commitment to Great Britain's survival in the war with Germany, could be extended to any nation including the U.S.S.R. whose defense the president deemed vital to American security. When Germany invaded Soviet territory on 22 June, the Roosevelt administration chose to help the U.S.S.R. but outside the Lend-Lease framework. Early opinion polls showed that Americans favored a Russian victory but not supplying war materiel to the U.S.S.R. on the same basis as Great Britain. The administration had to seek additional Lend-Lease funds from an uncertain Congress and did not want to jeopardize the program by adding the Soviet Union to its tally of Lend-Lease recipients.

TABLE 5

Sample U.S. Lend-Lease Exports to the U.S.S.R.		
(Actually Received at Soviet Destination)		
Item	Measure	Amount
Aircraft	Units	14,018
Automotive and Aviation Fuel	Tons	999,627
Cable and Wire	Miles	959,942
Cereals and Legumes	Tons	1,083,688
Dried Milk and Eggs	Tons	182,061
Explosives	Tons	325,784
Fats, Oils, Canned Meat	Tons	1,903,945
Field Telephones	Units	380,135
Motorcycles	Units	32,200
Radio Stations and Receivers	Units	41,699
Railway Cars and Locomotives	Units	13,041
Steel	Tons	2,121,730
Sugar	Tons	672,429
Tanks and Self-Propelled Guns	Units	12,161
Tools and Machinery	$1000	616,298
Trucks and Jeeps	Units	409,526
Weapons (Pistols, Mortars, etc.)	Units	136,190

Adapted from: Robert Huhn Jones. *The Roads to Russia: United States Lend-Lease to the Soviet Union.* Norman: University of Oklahoma Press, 1969.

Two days after the start of Russo-German hostilities, the U.S. Treasury Department released $39 million in Soviet assets that had been frozen, along with the assets of all

European nations, under an Executive Order issued just 10 days earlier. On 25 June, the White House announced that the Neutrality Act would not be invoked in the Nazi-Soviet conflict, leaving such Russian ports as Vladivostok open to American shipping. Before the end of June, Ambassador Umanskii made a formal request to the U.S. State Department for $1.83 billion worth of bombers, pursuit planes, aviation fuels and lubricants, anti-aircraft guns, ammunition, and industrial equipment. In July, President Roosevelt assured the U.S.S.R. of some American assistance in conferences with Umanskii and, through emissary Harry Hopkins, in talks with Stalin. Initially, Treasury Secretary Henry Morgenthau agreed in August to buy Soviet gold at the legal price of $35 per ounce and advanced the U.S.S.R. funds against future shipments. In September, Commerce Secretary Jesse Jones, via the Defense Supplies branch of the Reconstruction Finance Corporation, extended credit to Amtorg against later imports of a $100 million worth of Soviet manganese, chromium, platinum, and other products.

The U.S. government gradually adopted measures that foreshadowed aid through Lend-Lease. As early as July 1941, the Roosevelt administration transferred Russian procurement requests from the State Department to a special Soviet Supply Section in the Division of Defense Aid Reports, the agency supervising the Lend-Lease program. To coordinate Anglo-American production and the allocation of scarce war materiel, President Roosevelt and British Prime Minister Winston Churchill arranged with Stalin for a three-power conference that met in Moscow in late September. W. Averell Harriman, former concessionaire and board member of the American-Russian Chamber of Commerce, headed the U.S. delegation. He negotiated a secret protocol with Molotov and British Supply Minister Lord Beaverbrook. It listed discrete articles and detailed quantities of supplies that the U.S. and

Britain promised to make available to the Soviets by 30 June 1942.

The U.S. promised the Soviets $1 billion worth of equipment ranging from tanks to anti-tank guns. The agreement, however, only reopened and enlarged the financial problem that impeded the transfer of war materiel. Ever conscious of public opinion and the fragile consensus on Lend-Lease, FDR delayed the decision on helping the Soviets pay for this ordnance until Gallup polls revealed a favorable view toward Soviet aid and Congress approved a major appropriation for Lend-Lease. Another consideration in the decision-making process had to do with the Soviet response to the Wehrmacht's murderous assault. General Georgii Zhukov, who had distinguished himself in the border conflicts with Japan, took charge of the Moscow perimeter and under his leadership the Red Army stopped Hitler's forces a few miles from the city's outskirts. President Roosevelt chose this moment, of 30 October to offer the U.S.S.R. a billion-dollar, interest-free, Lend-Lease loan. The U.S. government waited to make the news public until 7 November 1941, the twenty-fourth anniversary of the Bolshevik Revolution.

The Japanese attack on Pearl Harbor thrust the U.S. into the global conflict and quickly changed the status of American-Soviet relations to one of a wartime alliance. The U.S.S.R. and U.S. signed a Master Agreement on 11 June 1942, that superseded previous financial arrangements and placed Lend-Lease assistance to the Soviet Union on a similar basis as Great Britain. The U.S. eventually furnished the U.S.S.R. with more than 17 million tons of supplies valued in excess of $10 billion. This massive transfer of war materiel occupied the central place in the economic relations of the two countries during the first half of the 1940s.

From the military standpoint, Lend-Lease made a valuable though not decisive contribution to the Soviet war effort. By 1944, many Soviet soldiers wore boots, ate food, fought in tanks, rode in trucks and "jeeps," and communicated over telephone wire supplied by the U.S. Hundreds of American vessels of various sizes and functions bolstered Soviet naval and merchant fleets and thousands of American aircraft suplemented the fighting capacity of the Soviet air force. American steel, aluminum, and copper went into the construction of Russian guns, tanks, aircraft, and ammunition. Tons of supplies moved into Soviet manufacturing centers over a train system repaired with American rails and improved by the addition of American locomotives and rolling stock. However, to put Lend-Lease in perspective, it did not exceed on a month-by-month basis 10% of Soviet production. Its full impact was not felt on the Eastern Front until the end of 1943, long after the Soviets had launched their successful counteroffensive. Finally, it was the Russian soldier, whether equipped by Soviet or American industry, who drove the Wehrmacht from Stalingrad to the streets of Berlin. The U.S.S.R. suffered wartime deaths between 14 and 20 million compared with 294,000 American deaths in World War II. Militarily, Lend-Lease provided Soviet soldiers with a transfusion of high-quality ordnance that permitted the Red Army to hasten the Third Reich's destruction. Ironically, though, in view of future events, Lend-Lease also strengthened the U.S.S.R. which, despite its losses, emerged from the crucible of war as a formidable military power in both Europe and Asia.[8]

NOTES

1. Quote from A. A. Gromyko, et. al., *Dokumenty vneshnei politiki SSSR*, Vol. 14 (Moscow: Gospolitizdat, 1968), 527; Condoide, *Russian-American Trade*, 91; Libbey, *Alexander Gumberg and Soviet-American Relations, 1917-1933*, 171-173. See also Robert C. Williams, *Russian Art and American Money, 1900-1940* (Cambridge: Harvard University Press, 1980).

2. Quote from chamber press release, 13 July 1933, Box 23, ARCC MSS.

3. Edward M. Bennett, *Franklin D. Roosevelt and the Search for Security: American-Soviet Relations, 1933-1939* (Wilmington: Scholarly Resources, 1985), 18-20; Frederick C. Adams, *Economic Diplomacy: The Export-Import Bank and American Foreign Policy, 1934-1939* (Columbia: University of Missouri Press, 1976), 70-72. See also Robert Paul Browder, *The Origins of Soviet-American Diplomacy* (Princeton: Princeton University Press, 1953); Maksim M. Litvinov, *Vneshniaia politika SSSR, rechi i zaiavleniia 1927-1937 gg.* (Moscow: Sotsekgiz, 1937).

4. Libbey, "Soviet-American Trade," 198; John Quigley, *The Soviet Foreign Trade Monopoly: Institutions and Laws* (Columbus: Ohio State University Press, 1974), 67; Smith, *Soviet Foreign Trade*, 70-71.

5. Bennett, *Franklin D. Roosevelt and the Search for Security*, 123-124. See also Thomas R. Maddux, *Years of Estrangement: American Relations with the Soviet Union, 1933-1941* (Tallahassee: University of Florida Press, 1980); Antony C. Sutton, *Western Technology and Soviet Economic Development 1930-1945* (Stanford: Hoover Institution, 1971).

6. Quote from Williams to Schley, 19 October 1939, Reeve Schley Papers, New Jersey Historical Society, Drawer 10.

7. Gaddis, *Russia, the Soviet Union, and the United States*, 142-143; Libbey, "The American-Russian Chamber of Commerce," 246-247; Maddux, *Years of Estrangement*, 124; Gerhard L. Weinberg, *Germany and the Soviet Union* (Leiden: Brill, 1954), 66-75.

8. George C. Herring, Jr., *Aid to Russia 1941-1946: Strategy, Diplomacy, the Origins of the Cold War* (New York: Columbia University Press, 1973), 32-48. See also Raymond H. Dawson, *The Decision to Aid Russia, 1941: Foreign Policy and Domestic Politics* (Chapel Hill: University of North Carolina Press, 1959); Robert Huhn Jones, *The Roads to Russia: United States Lend-Lease to the Soviet Union* (Norman: University of Oklahoma Press, 1969).

Chapter 4

BUILDING COLD WAR BARRIERS TO ECONOMIC RELATIONS

While American productive capacity increased, the Soviet Union's economy experienced a devastation that paralleled its human costs in World War II. The German invasion prompted an ancient Russian strategy: to destroy everything of military value in the path of advancing enemy divisions. Later, when the Red Army forced the Wehrmacht to abandon Soviet territory, the Nazis employed the same scorched-earth policy. The war turned 70,000 towns and villages into rubble including 6,000,000 buildings, 84,000 schools, 43,000 libraries, 31,000 factories, and 1,300 bridges. In the countryside, collective farms sustained the loss of 137,000 tractors, 49,000 harvesters, 7,000,000 horses, 17,000,000 cattle, 20,000,000 hogs, and 27,000,000 sheep and goats. Soviet authorities tend to exaggerate privations but it is reasonable to accept their estimate that half of Europe's war-related destruction occurred within Soviet boundaries.

THE SOVIET REQUEST FOR AMERICAN AID

On 3 January 1945, the Soviets formally asked the U.S. for a $6 billion line of credit to assist them in recovering from the terrible wartime destruction. Foreign Affairs Commissar Molotov placed the Soviet government's request in the hands of U.S. Ambassador Harriman. Simple pride or Communist bravado led Molotov to couch his note in ungracious terms. The Soviets took for granted that America's wartime production would lead to peacetime overproduction, and he insinuated that a U.S. loan would be in America's own interest. Soviet purchases, he theorized, would relieve the U.S. of surpluses thereby preventing the American economy from slipping into another depression. Moreover, Molotov urged favorable terms as a way of placing American-Soviet relations on a sound economic footing: the credit should run for 30 years at 2.25% interest with the first payment due in 1954.

It was not the tenor of Molotov's note but other diplomatic and domestic considerations that ultimately caused the U.S. to shunt aside his request for postwar aid. The key to America's response to the Soviet request lay in one of the great paradoxes to emerge at war's end. Despite the Soviet Union's pressing need for massive aid, it chose to surrender the good will of the U.S. and the other allies in order to pursue an independent policy. When the Third Reich collapsed in the spring of 1945, the Soviet Union replaced Germany as the controlling force in Eastern Europe. The U.S.S.R. adopted this role to prevent the region from serving again as an invasion route into the Russian heartland. Also, the opportunity to expand existed.

Premonitions that the Soviets planned to take charge of Eastern Europe's destiny appeared in the waning moments of 1944 when the U.S.S.R. excluded the West from political settlements in Romania and Poland—in part because it had been excluded from decisions regarding Italy. The Polish case strained the Grand Alliance because Britain and France had originally joined battle with Germany to preserve Polish independence. And the U.S. was concerned because it espoused democratic values and because it answered to six million American voters of Polish ancestry. On 1 January 1945, Stalin ignored FDR's personal plea and recognized the political authority of the Soviet-sponsored, Polish Committee of National Liberation.

Stalin later mollified Roosevelt and Prime Minister Churchill by his promise during the Yalta Conference (4-11 February 1945) to hold Polish elections. But even before Roosevelt's death on 12 April, Soviet behavior in Eastern Europe clouded American-Soviet relations. [1]

LEND-LEASE AND THE LEGACY OF ENMITY

America's strained ties with the Soviets, coupled with domestic pressures to limit spending, persuaded for President Harry Truman to stop the European phase of the Lend-Lease program just three days after hostilities had ceased. On 11 May 1945, he issued a directive that effectively cut all aid to the U.S.S.R. except for materials needed to complete construction projects already underway and for supplies deemed necessary to the Soviet Union in anticipation of the country's entrance into the war with Japan. The presidential directive produced an immediate halt in the loading of Soviet-bound ships in American harbors, and even led to the call-back of ships on the high seas. While the Soviets understood that Germany's surrender would eventually prompt a reduction in the Lend-Lease pipeline, they did not expect such an abrupt end to the assistance program. The Americans appeared to be applying "economic diplomacy" by insinuating that aid could be had—through a loan or some other mechanism—if only the Soviets would change their policies in Eastern Europe.

Because the cut-back affected other Lend-Lease recipients, the decision forced the Truman administration to admit that it had made a diplomatic blunder. The U.S. soon modified its policy and allowed ships being loaded and those at sea to proceed to their destinations.

The Truman administration failed to learn from these embarrassing experiences. U.S. officials chose once again to halt Lend-Lease shipments in the period between Emperor Hirohito's declaration of his nation's defeat on 14

August and Japan's formal surrender on 2 September. Indicative of the worsening relations between the U.S. and U.S.S.R., Lend-Lease personnel stopped Soviet shipments three days before they suspended aid to other recipients on 20 August. Again allied protests resulted in a resumption in the flow of Lend-Lease goods until 3 September, when the program finally ended. The U.S. offered the Soviets the same opportunity as the other allies to buy Lend-Lease supplies which had been ordered or manufactured by 3 September, but not yet shipped and they readily accepted. On 15 October 1945, the Soviets agreed to purchase $400 million worth of American goods that remained in the Lend-Lease pipeline with a nine-year grace period before they had to make the first of 22 annual payments at 2.38% interest.

Most products sent to the Soviet Union in the 14-month period after 15 October had been manufactured to Russian specifications, and the U.S. was happy to dispose of these otherwise unusable and unsalable stocks of supplies. Moreover, the agreement ultimately became another casualty of the rapidly developing Cold War era. Based on congressional legislation passed the next year, the U.S. Comptroller General ruled that pipeline deliveries had to end by 31 December 1946. The Truman administration, however, used legal technicalities to fulfill contracts signed with all Lend-Lease countries except the Soviet Union. Even though most pipeline articles had reached Soviet ports by the end of 1946, the premature termination of the agreement constituted a violation of America's contract with the Soviet government. This only complicated the general settlement of U.S. claims for the wartime lend-lease program.

Negotiations over these major claims began in 1947. American officials did not anticipate reimbursement for Lend-Lease supplies consumed in war but the Truman administration fully expected compensation for civilian goods, such as locomotives and industrial machinery, which had survived hostilities. Since the Soviets refused American requests for an inventory of Lend-Lease articles that remained intact and usable on V-J Day, the U.S. government could only guess their total value. It decided to halve its own estimate of $2.6 billion and agreed in 1948 to settle the Lend-Lease account for $1.3 billion. Arguing that Americans should basically forgive the debt out of consideration for the high casualties suffered by the Soviet people in World War II, the U.S.S.R. countered with a figure of only $170 million. By 1951, the Soviets had added $130 million to their 1948 offer while the Americans had dropped $500 million from their earlier demands. Secretary of State Dean Acheson expressed the administration's frustration over these drawn-out talks early in 1952: the Soviets must agree to American terms or join the U.S. in submitting the dispute to international arbitration. The Soviets spurned the ultimatum, creating an impasse that lasted for years.

A related problem, one interferring with the financial settlement, concerned the disposition of 711 American ships loaned to the U.S.S.R. under the Lend-Lease program. Although 585 of these vessels were small craft, e.g., torpedo boats, the fleet also included 96 freighters, 27 frigates, and three icebreakers. The U.S. asked the U.S.S.R. to return about 200 of these ships, suggesting that the remainder (declared surplus property) could be purchased on favorable terms. After several months, the U.S.S.R. transferred the frigates, icebreakers, and nine merchant ships to the U.S. and agreed to buy the remaining freighters and some of the small craft. Talks on the sale price for these ships dragged on for several years until finally, in 1951, the U.S. broke off negotiations and withdrew its offer to sell the ships. Between 1954 and 1956, the U.S.S.R. returned 127 small craft, sank another 90 inoperable vessels under observation of the U.S. Navy, and claimed that an additional 317 ships had been scrapped or were unserviceable. Nevertheless, the Soviet government neither paid nor accounted for 128 ships that presumably (in some cases, observably) continued to serve in its naval and merchant fleets for decades after World War II.[2]

THE ABORTIVE U.S. LOAN TO THE U.S.S.R.

While the U.S. set aside as extravagant Molotov's *aide-memoire*, it "lost" the Soviet government's more realistic application for a billion dollar loan. The head of the Soviet Purchasing Commission, General Leonid Rudenko, submitted a billion dollar loan proposal to the U.S. Foreign Economic Administration (FEA) on 28 August 1945. Created two years earlier, the FEA coordinated Lend-Lease and 19 other wartime agencies. The State Department, which had final approval on foreign aid, gave the application minimal attention. One reason for the low priority was that the Soviets failed to pursue their own request. Also, the Foreign Ministers Conference held in London in September, 1945 did further damage to U.S.-U.S.S.R. ties as America rejected Soviet peace treaties for several East European nations and refused the Soviets a role in the occupation of Japan. The U.S. government admitted in January 1946 that it had misplaced and mishandled the Soviet loan request and took immediate measures to rectify its error. But by then, President Truman's "get tough" policy with the Russians permeated the attitudes of his administration. As the Americans formulated their position on negotiations, there was little doubt that they intended to use the loan as leverage in extracting concessions. Indeed, the State Department's position paper of 21 February 1946, specified that projected loan talks must also resolve numerous issues, encompassing everything from a financial settlement for Lend-Lease to a U.S. role in Eastern Europe's recovery. When informed of these conditions in the spring, the Soviets expressed reluctance to deal with so many problems that appeared to be extraneous to the central question. Domestic politics and the administration's own rhetoric, then, helped persuade the U.S. government to interpret as unacceptable the Soviet response to American conditions for a loan.[3]

POLITICAL AND ECONOMIC CONTAINMENT OF THE U.S.S.R.

American anger at Soviet behavior finally coalesced in 1947 around a policy intended to contain the U.S.S.R. and prevent it from expanding further its influence. The cornerstone for America's new position was in President Truman's address before a joint session of Congress on 12 March 1947. In seeking funds for military and economic assistance to check Communist insurgents in Greece and Soviet military demands on Turkey, Truman suggested that any time free peoples are threatened by direct or indirect aggression it "undermines the foundation of international peace and hence the security of the United States."[4] The "Truman Doctrine" galvanized American political opinion around an anti-Communist consensus that dominated domestic politics and foreign relations for years to come. Congress quickly approved the first installment of $659 million that went to Greece and Turkey between 1947 and 1950.

The Greek-Turkish aid bill paved the way for Secretary of State George C. Marshall's 5 June 1947 proposal for European recovery. Justified on humanitarian grounds, the Marshall Plan also reflected America's concern for Western Europe's large Communist parties. They had garnered prestige in the struggle against Fascism and found strength in the economic wreckage left in the wake of war. The Marshall Plan thus became a logical extension of the Truman Doctrine. On the surface, the plan offered U.S. aid to all European nations, including the U.S.S.R., devastated by the recent conflict. In reality, it was designed to reduce communism's appeal, hence Soviet influence, in Western Europe by promoting economic stability. Once the Soviets rejected the Marshall Plan in July 1947, it guaranteed the division of Europe into East-West blocs. Subsequently, the U.S. pumped $12 billion in aid to 16 nations via the Organization for European Economic Cooperation, making a significant contribution to Western Europe's remarkable postwar recovery.[5]

CREATION OF U.S. TRADE CONTROLS

Foreign loans and assistance programs threatened to overtax American resources and justified President Truman's recommendation to Congress for the Second Decontrol Act passed in July 1947. The legislation gave the executive branch the authority to supervise approximately 20% of America's exports in broad categories related to foods, fuels, and metals. While the mechanism for curtailing exports was not directed specifically at the U.S.S.R., it contained the seeds for future punitive treatment. The bill had an immediate and adverse impact on American-Soviet trade because it required importing nations to file reports outlining current consumption, imports, production, and reserve stocks of those products desired from U.S. sources. Because the Soviets were reluctant to divulge economic data, they were denied access to a growing list of American goods. By the end of 1947, the U.S. no longer exported to the Soviet Union manufactured steel, railway equipment, or petroleum products including synthetic rubber.

The Soviets perceived American export controls as discrimination and responded with a measure designed to foster internal pressure against the U.S. government. In the fall of 1947, Amtorg announced that future contracts between American firms and Soviet import organizations would stipulate that unless Washington granted an export license by the time of shipment, the contract could be cancelled. Amtorg's notice produced an effect the opposite of the one intended. U.S. businessmen, already caught up in the country's anti-Soviet mood, became less eager to secure Russian orders. Export controls and uncertain contracts negatively influenced American-Soviet commerce which dropped nearly 50% from $226.1 million to $114.7 million between 1947 and 1948.

In February 1948, the U.S.S.R. backed a coup in Czechoslovakia that removed the last, semi-autonomous coalition government in the Soviet sphere. On the heels of this event, the Soviets challenged Western access rights to Berlin. The Czechoslovakian coup and the Berlin blockade provoked sharp restrictions on the shipment of American goods to the Soviet Union, restrictions based on political considerations rather than economic necessity.

Both sides wielded commerce like a sword in the Cold War struggle, striking blows and counterblows that left American-Soviet economic relations in tatters. The U.S.S.R. retaliated against U.S. export policies in December 1948 by curbing the sale of such items as manganese and platinum. These materials possessed strategic value by their use in armaments, aircraft, and communications equipment. The restrictions forced U.S. importers to make up their losses by scurrying into Third World markets. The Soviet reprisal encouraged Congress to approve a sweeping Export Control Act of February 1949. The legislation established, through the Department of Commerce, comprehensive licensing procedures for all exports, not just those going to Europe. It also created commodities lists to limit or prevent the sale and transfer of specific products or technologies that might enhance the strength of America's adversary. And in the confrontation over Berlin, American officials deemed most U.S. products of military value. By 1950, U.S. sales to the U.S.S.R. fell below a million dollars.[6]

SOVIET ALTERNATIVES AND THE FORMATION OF COMECON

Without significant forms of U.S. aid, the U.S.S.R. turned inward or looked to Eastern Europe for resources to assist with its economic recovery. Stalin and the Politburo resorted to a sequence of five-year plans to repair wartime damages and resume economic development. The Fourth Plan (1946-1950) resembled its earlier counterparts by its emphasis on basic industry. Approximately 85% of available capital flowed into the production of cement, coal, electricity, iron, lumber, steel, trucks, and agricultural machinery. Another significant element in the Soviet revival came from reparations—perhaps as much as $20 billion worth of material and equipment—collected from defeated Germany and its allies, Hungary and Romania. For economic as well as political reasons, the U.S.S.R. strengthened commercial ties with Eastern Europe by negotiating bilateral trade agreements and forming joint companies with the region's newly-created socialist governments.

The Soviet Union's military presence gave it an enormous advantage in terms of redirecting Eastern Europe's international commerce. Nevertheless, the U.S.S.R. experienced a decline in trade with several East European countries by 1947. And the Marshall Plan threatened to further erode the Soviet position as Czechoslovakia and Poland expressed interest in the American-sponsored program. Once the U.S.S.R. rejected participation in July, it also prohibited nations in her sphere from working with the West. On the other hand, the Marshall Plan did force the U.S.S.R. to shift economic gears. The U.S.S.R. supplied credits to Bulgaria, Czechoslovakia, and Yugoslavia and it forgave 50% of the reparations due from Hungary and Romania.

The Communist Information Bureau (Cominform), established in September 1947, united national Communist parties in Eastern Europe under Soviet leadership similar to the Third International, which had been disbanded by the Soviets as a good-will gesture toward its allies during World War II. The independently-minded Communist Party of Yugoslavia (CPY), however, questioned Soviet plans for the region, policies that consigned Eastern Europe to a subsidiary role. Yugoslavia rejected most Soviet offers for joint companies and created an autonomous and ambitious industrialization plan that challenged its assigned junior status. The Soviet Union encouraged Cominform to expel the CPY in June 1948. At it also ended trade with the Belgrade government (until 1953) and exerted pressure on other East European nations to follow suit. The Yugoslav incident revealed that Cominform was an inappropriate vehicle to assist in the Soviet drive to integrate economically Eastern Europe with the U.S.S.R. Thus in January 1949, representatives from Bulgaria, Czechoslovakia, Hungary, Poland, and Romania met in Moscow to found the Council for Mutual Economic Assistance (Comecon).* Albania and East Germany soon joined the organization although the former withdrew when it broke with Moscow in 1961.

Comecon devised a common strategy to enhance the reciprocal economic relations of member states, by seeking to coordinate national plans with existing specializations of the several socialist nations. Theoretically, this meant realigning foreign trade, perfecting exchange rates, and forming clearinghouses for the smooth transfer of products. A second public goal was to promote mutual aid to counteract the economic estrangement between East and West. Comecon would serve as an information center, sharing scientific and technical data to build or modernize the region's economic base. The First Comecon Session opened in Moscow on 26 April 1949. During the interim it established the Bureau of the Council, a Moscow-based apparatus to implement decisions and prepare agendas for Comecon's periodic gatherings. The Bureau was the forerunner of the contemporary Secretariat (1954) and Executive Committee (1962).

Political factors outweighed the economic reasons for Comecon's creation, and its welfare depended entirely on Soviet interest. The advent of the Korean War (June 1950) forced the Soviet bloc to devote its energies to nurturing traditional industries, especially those related to armaments, rather than fashioning a multinational socialist economy. That the Comecon's goals were too ambitious became obvious during the abbreviated Third Session of January 1950 when delegates could not agree on how to organize relations among centrally planned economies. Finally, key Soviet figures such as Stalin wavered between bilateralism and multilateralism in selecting an economic policy for Eastern Europe. While Comecon was later revived and would eventually play an important part in the region's economic development, it never lived up to the promise of its early publicity.[7]

EXTENSION AND EXPANSION OF U.S. TRADE CONTROLS

The Soviets dominated Eastern Europe's international commerce in a way similar to the position the U.S. held in Western Europe, though Americans exercised more subtly their instruments of coercion. The Marshall Plan alone bestowed on the U.S. considerable leverage to channel Europe's economic life in a manner that reflected the political dichotomy between East and West. In November 1949 France, Great Britain, Italy, and the Low Countries agreed to join the U.S. in founding the Consultative Group Coordinating Committee (CoCom). Membership in the unchartered and informal group was extended in 1950 to Canada, Denmark, Japan, Norway, Portugal, and West Germany, and in August 1953, Greece and Turkey joined the group. CoCom organized the West's economic boycott of the Soviet Union and its allies in Europe and Asia. The

United States' Mutual Defense Assistance Act or Battle Act in 1951, mandated the executive branch to withhold military and economic aid from any country that shipped strategic goods to a nation or group of nations that threatened U.S. security. Consequently, most American products denied the Soviet Union reappeared on CoCom's commodities list of embargoed items.

While the Truman administration orchestrated Western Europe's support for America's boycott, it promoted legislation that raised existing barriers in American-Soviet economic relations. The Korean War contributed to a stridently anti-Communist mood in Congress that favored a virtual end to trade with the U.S.S.R. The previously mentioned (see Chapter III) Trade Agreements Extension Act of 1951 withdrew most-favored-nation tariff treatment from the Soviet Union as well as from "any nation or area dominated or controlled by the foreign government or foreign organization controlling the world Communist movement."[8] A section within the same act barred seven Soviet furs from American shores: ermine, fox, kolinsky, marten, mink, muskrat, and weasel. Congress justified this unusual prohibition on the basis that it would keep the Soviets from acquiring American dollars, currency that would then be used to buy U.S. military hardware. Such a rationale made little sense in light of export controls and the Battle Act, not to mention that the Soviets were free to sell other products in the American market.

Common sense and logical behavior could not always compete with the anxiety and hatred that permeated American thinking toward the Soviet Union. Senator Joseph R. McCarthy, whose name became a sobriquet for this tragic era of fear, originally suggested the ban on Soviet furs. The Wisconsin senator mixed down-home politics with anti-Communist rhetoric in order to eliminate Soviet competition with his state's mink industry. Congress approved theTrade Agreements Extension Act without realizing that, except for muskrat, these Soviet furs were either unique to the American market or did not vie with American products. Moreover, such careless legislation had harmful effects on the American industry. First, it undermined New York City's position as the fur capital of the world. International buyers, who expected the widest selection of furs, shifted their patronage from New York to London where Russian furs were welcomed. Second, the decline in the New York fur trade soon forced over 600 dressing, dyeing, and manufacturing firms to close their doors with a consequent loss of thousands of American jobs.

In 1952, $16.8 million worth of Russian goods entered American ports compared with $86.8 million just four years earlier. The Cold War nadir in American-Soviet commerce was reached the following year, 1953, when the U.S. imported from the U.S.S.R. goods worth $10.8 million while exporting to the same country products valued at under twenty thousand dollars. Nevertheless, the U.S.S.R. chose to continue a small program of exports consisting of animal products and non-strategic minerals; as a result, the Soviet Union for the first time enjoyed a favorable balance of trade. This one-sided commercial activity netted the U.S.S.R. $280.4 million in American currency from 1948 through 1959. The Soviets partially applied this reserve to current and residual obligations for its purchases in America including payments on the Lend-Lease pipeline supplies of 1946.[9]

DECLINE OF THE SOVIET BOYCOTT

Soviet willingness to begin payments on its pipeline Lend-Lease debts in 1954 became one of several indicators that the U.S.S.R. had revised its economic and political policies following Stalin's death in March 1953. In the midst of the struggle among rival claimants to Stalin's position, the Soviet Union embarked on the so-called "New Course" which deemphasized rapid industrialization in favor of a more balanced economic growth. The government also relaxed its paternalistic behavior toward Eastern Europe, as Moscow resumed commercial relations with the outcast government in Belgrade and it reactivated Comecon. The Soviets also dismantled or sold numerous joint companies that had functioned in the dual role of promoting Russian political and economic interests in Eastern Europe.

TABLE 6

Sample Comparison of Soviet Trade with the West, 1947-1959					
(Total Turnover, in Millions of Dollars)					
Year	U.S.	U.K.	F.R.O.G.	France	Italy
1947	226.1	79.9	0.7	10.3	4.5
1948	114.7	130.4	2.0	11.3	7.6
1949	45.7	84.6	0.7	5.5	34.3
1950	39.0	128.3	0.2	7.6	34.7
1951	27.4	178.8	0.4	18.6	45.8
1952	16.8	173.5	4.2	25.2	54.5
1953	10.8	121.0	17.3	32.9	32.5
1954	12.0	145.3	34.8	70.6	50.0
1955	17.1	239.4	62.6	84.9	39.1
1956	28.3	228.0	121.4	104.7	49.2
1957	21.2	302.0	157.0	111.6	93.7
1958	20.9	232.9	164.2	170.4	70.9
1959	36.0	253.3	196.5	191.2	122.5

Adapted from: Gunnar Adler-Karlsson. *Western Economic Warfare, 1947-67*. Stockholm: Almquist &Wiksell, 1968; James H. Giffen. *The Legal and Practical Aspects of Trade with the Soviet Union*. Rev.Ed. New York: Praeger, 1971.

Business and political leaders in Western Europe, unlike Americans, were more flexible in their response to

Soviet and East European overtures for expanded commercial relations. In the spring of 1952, the U.S.S.R. sponsored an International Economic Conference attended by 200 Western businessmen who listened to Mikhail Nesterov, President of the U.S.S.R. Chamber of Commerce, call for a relaxation of the embargo that would enable the Soviets to initiate a major buying program in Western Europe. While the conference did not lead to changes in policy, it made businessmen more sensitive to the decline in the West's export trade with the East. Even American analysts admitted that the U.S.-inspired boycott annually cost CoCom nations nearly a quarter of a billion dollars in sales. Shortly after the Korean Truce, CoCom members urged the administration of President Dwight D. Eisenhower to reduce the list of embargoed goods. The CoCom nations agreed on 21 July 1954, to cut the international embargo list to under 200 items. This major American concession demanded in return greater surveillance and stricter control of the goods still denied the Communist bloc.

America adjusted its commodities list; however, it continued to embargo hundreds of items not controlled by its allies and still insisted that goods or technologies that would enhance the Soviet military must not be transferred. While U.S. exports to the U.S.S.R. rose to a trifling $4.4 million in 1957, other CoCom countries enjoyed a boom. Between 1953 and 1957, Italy's sales to the U.S.S.R. increased from $23.2 million to $42.4 million; France's sales nearly trippled from $16.0 million to $45.1 million; England's jumped from $9.3 million to $104.7 million; and even West Germany, a political pariah to Moscow, exported $59.6 million worth of products in 1957. By 1957, the Soviet bloc had negotiated over 200 trade agreements with CoCom nations. Soviet technological advances, as revealed by its hydrogen bomb and its space satellite, indicated to some Western observers the futility of trade controls.

Allied support for America's expansive definition of strategic materials fell in proportion to the diminishing effects of the embargo. CoCom members persuaded the U.S. to review the international list and produced a streamlined list of slightly more than 100 goods and technologies that was clearly focused on weaponry. The 1958 CoCom agreement signaled the end to an American-led, unified, Western economic policy toward the Soviet bloc as the U.S. embargoed nearly 700 commodities not found in the revised international list. The disparity in views between the U.S. and her allies measurably influenced commerce. England's total trade with the U.S.S.R. exceeded the quarter-billion-dollar mark in 1959 while America's trade barely reached $36 million and, characteristically for the 1950s, Soviet sales to the U.S. outdistanced its purchases by a ratio of four-to-one.[10]

AMERICAN CONSTRAINTS / SHIFTING SOVIET POLICIES

The narrow trade path America traveled during the latter half of the 1950s sharply contrasts with the twists and turns that distinguished Soviet policy. Nikita Khrushchev's notion of "peaceful coexistence" advanced Soviet communism as a global competitor to Western capitalism. Khrushchev's revisionist stance—ending the occupation of Austria and participating in Geneva disarmament talks—did not permit radical changes in Eastern Europe, as seen in the Soviet Union's suppression of the Hungarian revolt. Also peaceful coexistence did not lessen the competition in armaments, as *Sputnik's* launch in 1957 was accompanied by the successful test firing of a Soviet intercontinental ballistic missile. Looming over all these developments was Khrushchev's determination to settle the Berlin question on his terms.

In the bluff and bluster, vagaries and complexities posed by Khrushchev's diplomacy, nothing proved more baffling to the U.S. than his personal desire to improve American-Soviet relations. On 2 June 1957, the Soviet leader appeared on "Face the Nation," to urge the normalization of political ties by eliminating trade barriers and increasing cultural exchanges. Four days later, Moscow submitted a broad-scale proposal for cultural exchanges which the U.S. initially dismissed as propaganda. But Moscow's initiative caught the imagination of many Americans, if for no other reason than it presented an opportunity to expose the closed nature of Soviet society. U.S. Senate leaders Lyndon B. Johnson and J. William Fulbright persuaded the Eisenhower administration to at least reply to the Soviet note. The State Department's belated and tersely-worded, three-sentence message to the Kremlin resulted in a sweeping American-Soviet cultural exchange agreement signed on 17 January 1958. Among benefits for economic relations, the agreement promoted tourism, trade fairs, and reciprocal visits by industrialists and agronomists.

With success one area, Khrushchev sought the elimination or reduction in U.S. trade restrictions. He tried to influence American policy through personal correspondence with President Eisenhower in June 1958. But that failed. Throughout this period, America's response to the Soviet bid for improved commercial relations remained consistent. U.S. officials repeatedly claimed that trade restrictions delayed the Soviet Union's military build-up and hampered the country's material progress. Acting Secretary of Commerce Lewis Strauss, an avowed champion of trade controls, enlarged the embargo by adding copper commodities to America's restricted list in February 1959. And Congress enacted a measure to prohibit imports of Communist-built, classroom equipment. Similar to the case of furs, the ban resulted from a merger of anti-Communist sentiment with the desires of special interest groups.

When Khrushchev visited the U.S. in September 1959, America's negative stance on economic relations with the Soviets was, if anything, more firmly fixed than when the Soviet Premier broached the subject on American TV two years earlier. U.S. officials informed the Soviets that any change in trade laws required congressional cooperation and that this could only be accomplished by a settlement of differences in various areas such as Lend-Lease. The Soviets declined to consider Lend-Lease independently of a trade treaty, long-term credits, and other economic issues. Thus, the course of the Cold War witnessed a reversal in the positions held by the two nations; in 1959, the U.S.S.R. adopted the U.S. policy of 1946 of weaving various problems together into a single fabric. Yet the accumulated anti-Soviet attitudes in America were so deeply embedded that each administration could only effect change by addressing disputes in discrete steps. Indeed, the barriers impeding commerce were so solidly constructed during the Cold War that some of them would later prove to be inviolable despite changing conditions in American-Soviet relations.[11]

NOTES

1. John Lewis Gaddis, *The United States and the Origins of the Cold War 1941-1947* (New York: Columbia University Press, 1972), 189-194; Walter LaFeber, *America, Russia, and the Cold War, 1945-1966* (New York: Wiley, 1967), 14; Thomas G. Paterson, "The Abortive American Loan to Russia and the Origins of the Cold War, 1943-1946," *Journal of American History* 56 (June 1969), 70-92; Adam B. Ulam, *Expansion and Coexistence: The History of Soviet Foreign Policy, 1917-67* (New York: Praeger, 1968), 367-377. See also Viacheslav M. Molotov, *Voprosy vneshnei politiki, rechi i zaiavleniia 1945-1948 gg.* (Moscow: Gospolitizdat, 1948).

2. George C. Herring, Jr., "Lend-Lease to Russia and the Origins of the Cold War, 1944-1945," *Journal of American History* 56 (June 1969), 93-114. See also Herring, *Aid to Russia*, 296-301; Jones, *The Roads to Russia*, 69.

3. Thomas G. Paterson, *Soviet-American Confrontation: Postwar Reconstruction and the Origins of the Cold War* (Baltimore: Johns Hopkins University Press, 1973), 46-56.

4. Quote from *Public Papers of the Presidents of the United States: Harry S. Truman, 1947* (Washington, DC: GPO, 1963), 178.

5. Dean Acheson, *Present at the Creation: My Years in the State Department* (New York: Norton, 1969), 220-235; Mr. X [George F. Kennan], "The Sources of Soviet Conduct," *Foreign Affairs* 25 (July 1947), 566-582. See also Lloyd C. Gardner, *Architects of Illusion: Men and Ideas in American Foreign Policy 1941-1949* (Chicago: Quadrangle, 1970).

6. Paterson, *Soviet-American Confrontation*, 66-74; U.S. Department of Commerce, *Sixth Quarterly Report Under the Second Decontrol Act of 1947* (Washington, DC: GPO, January 1949), 12.

7. The best documented study on the origins and operations of Comecon is Jozef M. van Brabant, *Socialist Economic Integration: Aspects of Contemporary Economic Problems in Eastern Europe* (Cambridge: Cambridge University Press, 1980). See also Margaret Dewar, *Soviet Trade with Eastern Europe, 1945-1949* (London: Royal Institute of International Affairs, 1951); Il'ia V. Dudinskii, *Mirovaia sistema sotsializma* (Moscow: Sotsekgiz, 1961).

8. Quote from "Trade Agreements Extension Act of 1951," *U.S. Statutes at Large* 65, Section 5 (Washington, DC: GPO, 1952), 75.

9. David William Folts, "The Role of the President and Congress in the Formulation of United States Economic Policy Towards the Soviet Union, 1947-1968." Ph.D. Diss., University of Notre Dame, 1971, 79-81 and 163-165; Marshall I. Goldman, *Detente and Dollars* (New York: Basic Books, 1975), 55; Paul Y. Hammond, *Cold War and Detente: The American Foreign Policy Process Since 1945* (New York, Harcourt, 1975), 55-56.

10. *New York Times*, 6 April 1952; Nicholas Spulber, "Effect of the Embargo on Soviet Trade," *Harvard Business Review* 30 (November/December 1952), 122-128; Harold Stassen, "Revision of Strategic Trade Controls," *Mutual Defense Assistance Control Act of 1951, Fifth Report to Congress* (Washington, DC: GPO, November 1954); Douglas Dillon, "The 1958 Revision of East-West Trade Controls," *Mutual Defense Assistance Control Act of 1951, Twelfth Report to Congress* (Washington, DC: GPO, April 1959). See also Suchati Chuthasmit, "The Experience of the United States and Its Allies in Controlling Trade with the Red Bloc, 1948-1960." Ph.D. Diss., Fletcher School of Law and Diplomacy, 1961.

11. Folts, "The Role of the President and Congress," 123-129; J. D. Parks, *Culture, Conflict and Coexistence: American-Soviet Cultural Relations, 1917-1958* (Jefferson: McFarland, 1983), 165-171.

Chapter 5

COLLAPSE OF THE AMERICAN CONSENSUS ON SOVIET TRADE

The "spirit of Camp David," proved to be a brief respite between crises over Berlin and the U-2 affair. The latter incident in May 1960, led to the cancellation of both a summit conference on Berlin and President Eisenhower's trip to Moscow. The renewed Cold War tensions obscured in the West the basic thrust of Khrushchev's search for accommodation. That the program was better understood among Communists was evident in gatherings of national parties in Bucharest and Moscow during 1960. China and Albania questioned Khrushchev's notion of peaceful coexistence and sharply censured the Soviet Premier for his failure to aid Third World revolutions. These private squabbles soon spilled into the public domain and made a mockery of Moscow's pretensions of directing a monolithic, international Communist movement. The Sino-Soviet conflict also aroused the CPSU's Politburo and Central Committee which expected Khrushchev to deflect China's assault on Moscow's supremacy. One result was Soviet military and economic aid to Fidel Castro's revolution in Cuba.

KENNEDY'S ECONOMIC POLICY

Ironically, as pressures shoved Khrushchev toward a confrontational position with the West, and especially with the U.S., the new American president, John F. Kennedy, indicated he would be more flexible in dealing with the Soviet Union and its allies. He reversed President Eisenhower's ban on Soviet crabmeat, a largely symbolic gesture. During his 1961 State of the Union message, JFK asked Congress for new "economic tools to help reestablish historic ties of friendship between the United States and the peoples of Eastern Europe."[1] And, finally, he appointed a study group headed by Under Secretary of State George Ball to explore issues related to East-West commerce. The study group urged major changes in the "almost completely negative policy toward trade with Communist nations."[2] Kennedy's drive for flexibility was genuine. Unlike his predecessor, Kennedy challenged the anti-Communist lobby in Congress in order to reassert the prerogatives of the executive branch in formulating American economic policy.

In the struggle between president and Congress, the latter won most battles. The House refused in 1961 to act on an administration-backed amendment to the Battle Act, which would have allowed the executive branch to provide economic assistance to Communist countries whenever it was in America's interest. Next year, when the Export Control Act came up for renewal, JFK unsuccessfully sought to make the legislation permanent so as to avoid the biannual Congressional review of the administration's trade control policies. In the wake of the abortive Bay of Pigs invasion of Cuba and the Soviet construction of the Berlin Wall, the revised Export Control Act embodied some of the most restrictive language in the Cold War era. It listed Communist countries by name and authorized the government to deny those nations exports of "economic" or military value. It prohibited American aid to countries supplying goods or shipping to Cuba. And in the misnamed Trade Expansion Act of 1962, Congress interferred with the president's efforts to undermine Soviet influence over Eastern Europe by withdrawing most-favored-nation tariff treatment from Yugoslavia and Poland. The latter so patently violated American self-interest that Congress corrected its error in 1963.

While Kennedy wrestled with Congress to create a more responsive, opportunistic economic policy toward Communist nations, he also tried to reclaim U.S. leadership over the West's trade relations with the East. The growth in Soviet petroleum sales to Western Europe concerned both the Eisenhower and Kennedy administrations because some of America's allies might come to depend on Soviet oil and hence be subject to Soviet influence during East-West confrontations. American oil companies were alarmed though for different reasons. Soviet competition prompted the National Petroleum Council to lobby for a continuation of the U.S.'s export ban on petroleum-connected equipment or technology to the Soviet Union. Matters came to a head in the early 1960s with the proposed construction of the Druzhba (Friendship) Oil Pipeline from the U.S.S.R. to Eastern Europe. Not only would the completed project facilitate Soviet petroleum sales in the West, but it would increase the strategic supply of fuels to Warsaw Pact military units, the Communist bloc's equivalent to NATO.

The Kennedy administration learned that the Druzhba project had run into difficulty because of an inadequate domestic supply of wide-diameter steel pipe, which the U.S.S.R. intended to remedy through major purchases in West Germany. These plans disturbed the U.S. government which, skirting CoCom, persuaded the NATO Council on 25 November 1962 to recommend that its members withhold wide-diameter steel pipe from the Soviet Union. The recommendation caused bitter debate within West Germany and weakened the Adenauer government. But not all NATO members shared America's concern over Soviet oil. Great Britain, for example, defied the U.S. by arranging to buy Russian oil and studying the possibility of building ships for Moscow in exchange for even larger petroleum allotments. Since the embargo did not stop the

Druzhba project and only promoted dissension within NATO, the Council subsequently withdrew its recommendation.[3]

U.S. GRAIN SALE TO THE U.S.S.R.

Understandably, the U.S. government originally pursued the embargo on wide-diameter steel pipe in the midst of the 1962 Cuban Missile Crisis. That superpower confrontation sobered the leaders of both governments, prompting them to seek to lessen the possibility of nuclear war. One result was the installation of the so-called "hot-line" that opened direct communications between the White House and the Kremlin. Despite objections from Peking, Moscow pressed for limited détente with the West as illustrated by its joining the U.S. and Great Britain in signing a limited nuclear test ban on 5 August 1963. The Soviet Union also agreed to endorse a United Nations resolution banning nuclear weapons from outer space. President Kennedy encouraged this trend in better relations when drought-related shortfalls in Soviet grain production forced the U.S.S.R. to seek purchase agreements for cereals in 1963.

The Canadian government informed the Kennedy administration of the preliminary negotiations and terms of its sale of $500 million worth of wheat and wheat flour to the Soviet Union. Ottawa officials emphasized that due to poor harvests in Europe and commitments to other markets, Canada could not supply all the wheat sought by the Russians. JFK subsequently offered American grain to the Soviet Union. Not only did the Soviets express favorable interest in buying U.S. wheat, but volunteered employing American vessels to ship the grain. On 9 October 1963, Kennedy informed the public of these discussions and tried to defuse domestic criticism of his initiative by downplaying the political significance of a trade agreement and highlighting the economic benefits of such a sale. He argued that the grain transfer would help several sectors of the American economy, improve the balance of trade payments and reduce the amount of surplus cereals being stored at taxpayers' expense.

While the president expected controversy, he was surprised by the breadth of Congressional opposition. Vice President Lyndon B. Johnson, former Senate Majority Leader, was one of the few administration members to assess correctly the transaction's political troubles. At the outset, the wheat deal became a partisan issue, but several Democrats who opposed trade with the Soviet Union soon joined Republicans in criticizing Kennedy. This opposition focused on the planned use of the U.S. Export-Import Bank to guarantee credit arrangements between American banks and the Soviet Union. Preliminary discussions between Americans and Russians paralleled the Canadian arrangement: the Soviets promised 25% cash payment for the grain with the balance to be paid in three equal installments at six-month intervals. Legislation introduced by Senator Karl Mundt of South Dakota and supported by other critics would prohibit the government and specifically the Export-Import Bank from guaranteeing "the payment of any obligation heretofore or hereafter incurred by any Communist country.in connection with the purchase of grain or any product thereof by such country, agency, or national."[4]

After Kennedy's assassination on 22 November 1963, the new chief executive, Johnson, fulfilled the programs begun by his predecessor, including the agreement to sell wheat to the Soviet Union. A master of legislative detail and skilled in bending the political system to his will, Johnson encouraged his Senate allies to submit the Mundt bill on the morning of Kennedy's funeral. Linking opposition to the measure with the residual sympathy many Senators held for JFK, he persuaded nine Democrats and one Republican to switch their support and defeat the bill. Meanwhile, the Export-Import Bank authorized $200 million in credit insurance for the benefit of the Soviet Union. The U.S.S.R., however, avoided further controversy over credit arrangements and saved interest costs by paying $149.8 million in gold for 65.6 million bushels of wheat and a lesser amount of rice.

Transportation, not financing, proved to be the final stumbling block to the grain deal. The Soviet purchasing delegation on 21 October 1963, voiced concern over American shipping firms charging several dollars more per ton of cargo than their maritime rivals. Moreover, the large size and deep draft of many U.S. vessels prohibited them from using Soviet port facilities. The U.S.S.R. thus balked at its own suggestion of hiring mainly American ships to carry the wheat. Subsequent American-Soviet talks were complicated by the reaction of various countries to the preference of the U.S. for American ships. On 7 November, ten European nations plus Japan protested the discriminatory shipping arrangements under discussion in Washington. Subsequently, the Americans and Russians hammered out a compromise "understanding" that U.S. freighters would ship 50% of the grain. On this basis, the Soviets completed transactions for wheat and rice with Cargill and the Continental Grain Company in January and February 1964.

The Soviets paid cost, insurance, and freight, and made the two U.S. companies responsible for implementing the American-Soviet accord. But Continental Grain found that it could not engage a sufficient number of U.S. freighters, and the American firm had to seek a waiver of the 50% rule. The U.S. Maritime Administration agreed with Continental that the percentage of American ships carrying Soviet wheat should be cut to thirty-eight percent.. This decision enraged Thomas W. Gleason, president of the International Longshoremen's Association. ILA members had already vented their anti-Communist feelings through wildcat boycotts against the loading of Soviet-bound ships. Gleason now threatened to convert these local boycotts into

ILA-sanctioned activities. President Johnson intervened personally and secured a compromise agreement: the ILA would load ships and in return the U.S. government would uphold the 50% rule in the future and urge the U.S.S.R. to accept larger U.S. vessels at its ports.[5]

BUILDING BRIDGES TO THE EAST

President Johnson and his advisers adopted the most positive attitude toward East-West trade of any administration since the advent of the Cold War. In a May 1964 tribute to the late George C. Marshall, Johnson spoke of using commerce to build bridges to the Communist nations. A variety of reasons stimulated this shift in viewpoint. First, Johnson, like Kennedy, looked for areas of cooperation with the U.S.S.R. to avoid confrontations such as the one over Cuba. Second, the administration grasped the advantages of a partial decline of Moscow's authority over the Communist movement resulting from the clash between Moscow and Peking.

The revised model of the Communist world contained polycentric and nationalistic components. With this situation in mind, President Johnson encouraged Americans to reexamine East-West economic ties. His political friends in Congress took up the "building bridges" theme during Senate Foreign Relations Committee hearings in the spring of 1964. Cabinet officials, bankers, industrialists, and academics testified in favor of a sophisticated policy that would deal with individual Communist nations and would employ trade to advance America's interests. The hearings, coupled with the administration's pro-trade rhetoric, altered the public attitudes of some business leaders. Until 1964, U.S. companies refrained from advocating trade with Communist nations for fear of being blacklisted. Now, prestigious business groups such as the National Foreign Trade Council and U.S. Chamber of Commerce endorsed East-West trade and called for a reevaluation of U.S. export controls. After all, the policy that had denied goods to the Soviet Union also denied profits to U.S. companies. In the year before the wheat sale, the total American-Soviet trade amounted to only $44.0 million, a low figure when compared with the lively commerce the Soviets conducted with West Germany ($317.6 million) and Great Britain ($409.8 million).

TABLE 7

Sample Comparison of Soviet Trade with the West, 1960-1971				
(Total Turnover, In Millions of Dollars)				
Year	U.S.	U.K.	F.R.O.G.	France	Italy
1960	61.8	313.6	345.5	210.3	205.5
1961	68.7	355.5	346.0	207.2	241.2
1962	36.2	352.9	392.7	248.8	270.1
1963	44.0	409.8	317.6	205.3	291.7
1964	166.9	382.0	365.0	205.0	238.0
1965	87.6	461.6	357.0	218.0	279.4
1966	91.1	492.9	380.6	247.6	279.2
1967	101.3	515.4	462.9	342.4	399.6
1968	115.7	624.0	567.0	439.3	463.5
1969	161.0	706.4	741.0	470.3	531.3
1970	195.5	773.2	764.0	476.5	589.4
1971	227.7	728.9	826.0	515.8	591.9

Adapted from: See Table 6 and Bruce Parrott, ed. *Trade, Technology, and Soviet-American Relations*. Bloomington: Indiana University Press, 1985.

President Johnson pursued the building bridges concept in his 1965 State of the Union Address as he promised to investigate the use of trade to promote "peaceful understanding" with Communist adversaries. In February, he appointed J. Irwin Miller, head of Cummins Engine Company, to chair a special committee on America's commercial relations with the Soviet Union and Eastern Europe. Later that year, the Miller Committee reported that the "time was ripe" to expand America's economic ties, concluding: "The intimate engagement of trade...can influence the internal development and external policy of European Communist societies along the paths favorable to our purpose and to world peace."[6] Johnson, in welcoming the Miller Committee's endorsement, allowed the discussion on East-West trade to focus narrowly on the political rather than the economic benefits such trade might bring.

Although he had the support of some business groups, he found it difficult to build a congressional consensus around his trade idea. The debate joined on whether it was more effective to use trade as a reward or a punishment to influence the behavior of Communist nations. This became obvious when the White House sought to implement one of the Miller Report's recommendations. On 3 May 1966, Johnson transmitted a proposed bill to Congress, allowing the president to extend most-favored-nation tariff treatment to Communist countries (except China, Cuba, East Germany, North Korea, and North Vietnam) whenever the chief executive determined that it was in the national interest. Unfortunately, tariff laws originate in the House Ways and Means Committee, the same panel responsible for suspending most-favored-nation tariff treatment from Poland and Yugoslavia in 1962. Chaired by Representative Wilbur D. Mills, the Ways and Means Committee killed the legislation. Mills' revolt against the leader of his own party can be understood within the context of the Vietnam War. To Mills and other politicians it seemed contradictory to offer economic favors to Communist nations providing arms to America's foes in Southeast Asia. The Johnson administration could ill afford to hold such simplistic views.

Far from diminishing the drive toward economic detente, the Vietnam War added another compelling reason for President Johnson to pursue his building bridges concept. It might provide the White House with the alternative of using trade to gain East European or Soviet aid in extricating the U.S. from the Asian war. Johnson refused to permit the House Ways and Means Committee to obstruct his policy, and he instructed the Department of Commerce to remove export controls from hundreds of nonstrategic items resulting in an immediate 30% jump in U.S. sales to the Soviet Union. He also supported American-Soviet talks on a civil air agreement and he encouraged the Export-Import Bank to guarantee commercial credit to four more Communist countries: Bulgaria, Czechoslovakia, Hungary, and Poland. Finally, in a speech on 7 October 1966, the president indicated that he would ask the Export-Import Bank to help finance the sale of American machinery for a new Soviet automobile plant being built with Fiat's help at Togliatti, a Soviet town named in honor of Italian Communist leader Palmiro Togliatti.[7]

FIAT AND THE FAILURE OF LBJ'S PROGRAM

The Italian firm and the Soviet Union contracted on 15 August 1966 for Fiat's assistance in building a plant with an annual capacity for 660,000 units. Fiat would engineer the production process, specify the type and source of the $550 million worth of Western machinery, train Soviet technicians to operate the equipment, and sell the rights to the Fiat 124 that would become the prototype for the vehicles manufactured at the Togliatti plant. At the time the contract was signed, the Soviet passenger car industry produced few cars relative to the size of the nation and possessed a level of technology far below its Western counterparts. Soviet models, such as the Moskvich, had a reputation as the most inferior automobiles in the world.

Soviet planners designed a 15-year program (1966-1980) to improve the quality and quantity of trucks, buses, and passenger cars. In the first phase automobile production would increase from 200,000 units in 1966 to 1.2 million in 1975. Along with an agreement with Renault of France to revamp two plants manufacturing a new Moskvich model, the Fiat arrangement enabled the U.S.S.R. to meet its goal. When the 15-year program ended, the Soviets annually produced 1.3 million automobiles. These major projects spawned a host of lesser contracts for the infusion of Western technology into vendor plants that furnished parts to the main assembly facilities. The West Germans built a car seat factory and the Japanese equipped an oil/air filter plant. Meanwhile, trade restrictions excluded U.S. companies from a primary role in the modernization and expansion of the U.S.S.R.'s automotive industry. Only President Johnson's reduction of export controls on selected goods permitted corporate America to serve as a supplier to West European firms holding Soviet contracts.

The White House balanced its concerns over this massive transfer of Western technology against the advantages of encouraging the U.S.S.R. to reallocate resources away from military hardware and toward consumer products. The Eighth Five-Year Plan (1966-1970) called for a 43-46% increase in consumer goods. The American theory, that as the Soviets made more butter they would build fewer guns, proved false on a relative basis. Events in Southeast Asia had an unanticipated effect on the Soviet's achievement of ICBM parity—not so much because the U.S.S.R. devoted huge amounts of national income to strategic arms but because the U.S. did not. President Johnson tried to ameliorate this situation with economic and political policies aimed at détente with the Soviets. His friendly discussions with Alexis Kosygin at

Glassboro, New Jersey, in 1967 were followed by the Nuclear Non-Proliferation Treaty signed on 1 July 1968. The same summer American and Soviet officials agreed to open arms control talks in Moscow in October, but, during the interim, the Soviet invasion of Czechoslovakia prompted Johnson to shelve plans for further negotiations with the Russians.

The Soviet power play in Czechoslovakia reinforced the long-held, anti-Soviet attitudes of the new President, Richard M. Nixon, who stridently opposed the expansion of economic relations with Communist nations. Nixon soon spoke out against any relaxation in trade restrictions. His administration had an early opportunity to back these words with action when the U.S.S.R. laid the foundation in 1969 for the second or truck phase of the 15-year modernization program for road vehicles. The Soviets needed large doses of Western technology if they were to produce 150,000 diesel trucks annually. Ford Motor and Mack Trucks entered preliminary talks with Soviet representatives for technical assistance agreements on trucks similar in scope to the contracts signed with Fiat and Renault for passenger cars. The Nixon administration, however, refused to give prior assurances on export licenses, forcing the American companies to back out of these discussions.[8]

THE MAIN FACTORS LEADING TO DÉTENTE

When in the summer of 1971, the U.S. lifted restrictions on the export of trucks and truck technology to the U.S.S.R. it was in response to a significant change in Soviet-American relations. Within months after taking the oath of office, President Nixon realized that he would have to abandon his rigid ideological position in order to deal effectively with the major problems confronting the nation. Among concerns facing Nixon were the U.S. disengagement from Vietnam and the American response to Soviet achievements in strategic weapons, including the deployment of an anti-ballistic missile system (ABM). At the suggestion of national security adviser, Henry A. Kissinger, the administration offered the Soviets expanded trade in return for help in opening peace talks with North Vietnam. Thus Nixon, who had criticized the measure, signed into law the Export Administration Act in December 1969, a month after American and Russian representatives opened the Strategic Arms Limitation Talks (SALT). The new export control law increased non-military trade with the Soviet Union and Eastern Europe. It removed controls on goods and technologies that were available to Communist countries from sources other than the U.S., consequently, by 1971, U.S. sales to the U.S.S.R. climbed to $166.0 million, nearly three times the 1968 figure.

Meanwhile, detente became as much a necessity as a virtue for the Soviets. Friction with the Chinese in 1969 reached beyond the normal exchange of public insults as Chinese and Soviet military forces engaged in pitched battles along the Ussuri River. With this provocative situation in mind, the U.S.S.R. strove to mend its fences with the West in order that any Far Eastern conflagration not trigger a response from NATO. In 1970, the Soviets signed a treaty with West Germany confirming the Oder-Neisse boundary and joined the other occupying powers in a 1971 accord normalizing Berlin's status. They also fostered contacts between the Warsaw Pact and NATO looking toward negotiations for a mutual and balanced reduction of armed forces. This "linkage" between American-Soviet, European-Soviet détente and China was not lost on Washington. President Nixon welcomed reconciliation with China at the same time that he pursued cooperation with the Soviets. Not long after Nixon received an invitation to visit Peking in 1971, the Soviets suggested an American-Soviet summit in Moscow. The projected summit stimulated the SALT talks to reach a satisfactory conclusion.

The Soviet government's concern with China was matched by its anxiety over the nation's material progress. Soviet leaders recognized in the later 1960s that their entire domestic economy was in serious trouble. Its sluggish pace stemmed from outmoded equipment as well as the dysfunctions inherent in a bureaucracy-laden society. Once Leonid Brezhnev assumed total control in 1969, his administration chose to attack the most visible problems in the economy such as food shortages and the East-West technology gap. The Soviet hierarchy found it easier to substitute Western commerce for major internal reforms. Moreover, improved economic ties with the West had long been advanced by the Soviets because of their conviction that expanded trade created within the industrial democracies a vested interest in peace.

Trade statistics indicate the priority assigned to the new policy. Between 1969 and 1979, Soviet purchases from the industrialized West plus Japan ballooned 843% as measured in dollar amounts, increasing from $2.3 billion to $19.4 billion. The annual value of U.S. exports to the U.S.S.R. rose at incredible rates, peaking at $3.6 billion in 1979 and vaulting the U.S. to second place (after West Germany) as the most important source of foreign products for the Soviets. Nevertheless, West Germany, Japan, France, and Italy supplied the U.S.S.R. with more high technology goods than did the United States because of self-imposed restrictions. The bulk of U.S. exports came from farms not factories as American grain was as vital to Russian needs. Unfavorable weather conditions, poor storage facilities, an inadequate transporation system, and the inefficiencies of collectivized agriculture combined to create a chronic grain shortage. In 1971, the CPSU approved a new economic program that for the first time since 1928 emphasized quality over quantity and consumer goods over heavy industry. The Ninth and Tenth Five-Year Plans (1971-1980) also allocated huge sums, five billion dollars in 1975-76 alone, for the acquisition of foreign grain, meat, and butter. A foretaste of later activity occurred in November 1971 when the Soviets bought $125 million worth of American wheat.[9]

DÉTENTE

With plans for purchasing Western food and technology firmly in place, the Soviets were eager to cement the SALT I accords—limiting defensive and offensive missiles—with a broad-based understanding on improved economic relations. At the 1972 Moscow Summit, the two nations signed a convention that encouraged links between U.S. firms and Soviet enterprises in the areas of science and technology. Shortly thereafter, a joint Soviet-American Commercial Commission was formed to monitor economic contacts and negotiate a trade agreement. Brezhnev and Nixon consented to the "Basic Principles of Relations" on 29 May, that symbolized and defined detente. The seventh principle held that "the USA and the USSR regard commercial and economic ties as an important and necessary element in the strengthening of their bilateral relations and thus will actively promote the growth of such ties."[10]

In the halcyon days after the Moscow summit, the two governments sought to fulfill the seventh principle. They approved a three-year arrangement on 8 July for the transfer of up to $750 million in American grain to the Soviet Union. Later that month, the first session of the Joint U.S.—U.S.S.R. Commercial Commission was held in Moscow. By October, when the second session convened in Washington, the group had hammered out a Maritime Agreement opening 40 ports in each country to the vessels of the other. More importantly, the commission reached a consensus on a comprehensive trade package. The Russians acknowledged their World War II Lend-Lease debt and promised to pay $722 million in return for the Nixon administration's pledge to seek Export-Import Bank credits for financing Soviet purchases in America and to gain Congressional approval for most-favored-nation tariff treatment for Soviet imports. At the same time, American businessmen and Soviet officials incorporated the U.S.— U.S.S.R. Trade and Economic Council in New York on 5 September 1973. Patterned on the Franco-Soviet Chamber of Commerce, the Council's unique feature was its binational structure that extended from top to bottom. Co-presidents superintended Council affairs: Harold B. Scott, former Assistant Secretary of Commerce; George S. Schukin, former head of the Kama Purchasing Commission that let contracts with American firms for the Soviet truck plant. Even the Board of Directors had an equal number of American and Soviet participants and all the specialized committees, ranging from finance to tourism, had dual leadership. The Council's unconventional structure corresponded to the extraordinary nature of its membership. Every key Soviet group with a role in foreign commerce, from FTOs to Gosplan, joined the Council. And the 250 U.S. companies affiliated with the organization by the mid-1970s had annual sales exceeding $325 billion or about 25% of the U.S. Gross National Product.

No direct link connected the American-Russian Chamber of Commerce with the Council but many firms represented on the board of directors of the defunct chamber exercised the same leadership in the new organization: American Express, Armco Steel, Chase Manhattan (formerly Chase National), General Electric, IBM Corporation (formerly International Business Machines), and International Harvester (now Navistar). Agribusiness accounted for only 10% to 15% of American participation in the Council's work since a small number of U.S. grain dealers satisfied the U.S.S.R.'s huge demand. The remainder came from America's largest and most important industrial and financial corporations.

TABLE 8

American-Soviet Trade, 1972-1980			
(In Millions of Dollars)			
Year	US Cereal Exports	Other US Exports	Total Imports	Total Turnover
---	---	---	---	---
1972	430	112	96	638
1973	921	274	2201	415
1974	300	307	350	957
1975	1,133	700	254	2,087
1976	1,487	819	221	2,527
1977	1,037	586	2341	,857
1978	1,687	562	540	2,789
1979	2,855	749	873	4,477
1980	1,047	463	453	1,963

Adapted from: U.S. Department of Commerce. *Highlights of U.S. Export and Import Trade.* Washington, DC: GPO, 1982.

These corporations joined because sales of non-agricultural goods rose 731% from $112 million to $819 million between 1972 and 1976. Another reason the Council gained prestigious members is that the Soviets courted major companies with heavy investments in research and development such as du Pont and Xerox. And the U.S.S.R. whetted the appetite of the entire business community by its well-publicized activity in the American market. Swindell-Dressler signed a multi-million dollar contract to design and equip the foundry for the Kama River Truck Plant. Occidental Petroleum, chaired by former concessionaire Armand Hammer, concluded a complicated 20-year, 20-billion dollar agreement with the Soviets in April 1973. Occidental exchanged technical assistance in the construction of ammonia factories and related facilities for a good price on the fertilizer produced by these plants.[11]

THE JACKSON-VANIK AMENDMENT AND DÉTENTE'S DECLINE

As American business mobilized for expanded trade with the Soviets, Congress generated a countervailing force. In October 1972, Democrat Senator Henry Jackson authored an amendment to a trade bill that tied the U.S.S.R.'s emigration policy to President Nixon's request for most-favored-nation tariff treatment for the Soviet Union. Republican representative Charles Vanik introduced a similar measure in the House, creating the Jackson-Vanik Amendment that altered the future course of American-Soviet economic relations. The amendment gained widespread support because it appealed to conservatives, who opposed any growth in Soviet commerce, and to liberals, who criticized Soviet conduct toward Jews and dissidents. The Nixon administration viewed trade agreements as an important tactic in a broad strategy to modify Soviet behavior in world affairs; congressional adherents to the Jackson-Vanik Amendment linked the lower tariff to a specific change in Soviet domestic policy, i.e., to Jewish emigration.

On one level the executive and legislative conflict seemed an extension of the clashes begun during the Kennedy administration; however, two characteristics distinguished the situation in the 1970s from the one in the 1960s. First, the amendment prompted the National Association of Manufacturers, U.S. Chamber of Commerce, National Foreign Trade Council, and U.S.—U.S.S.R. Trade and Economic Council to lobby against congressional strings on tariff concessions. These associations advanced the idea, alien to White House and Capitol Hill alike, that Soviet commerce was as much an economic matter as a political issue and that long-term governmental interference in foreign trade had left the U.S. with a tarnished reputation. To the advantage of America's competitors, export controls and politicized tariffs had made the U.S. an unreliable trading partner in world commerce.

Second, the Watergate scandal shadowed the White House and dimmed the power of its occupant. Nixon resigned from office in August 1974, leaving behind the unresolved trade controversy. His successor, Gerald R. Ford, retained the services of Henry Kissinger and pursued Nixon's goal of building "constructive relationships" with the Soviets. Ford met with Brezhnev at Vladivostok in November and accepted the framework for another arms control agreement that would eventually serve as a basis for SALT II. In the fall of 1974, Kissinger passed on to American politicians Soviet assurances that a stipulated number of Jews would be allowed to emigrate. Following an exchange of letters between Kissinger and Senator Jackson that spelled out the details on Jewish emigration, Congress and the administration worked out an agreement that empowered the president to grant tariff relief and government credits to the Soviet Union for an initial 18-month period.

On 20 December 1974, Congress completed its part of the bargain by approving two pieces of legislation. The Trade Act offered tariff concessions to the U.S.S.R. in exchange for emigration quotas on Soviet Jews. And the Export-Import Bank Amendment opened a $300 million line of credit for Soviet trade, but only if funds were not used for energy-related goods and technologies. Both measures met with disfavor in Moscow. The Soviets had not expected their private understandings with Secretary of State Kissinger to reappear in public law. Moreover, the qualifications attached to U.S. credits struck at the heart of the Soviet Union's economic program. The U.S.S.R. intended to pay for a significant portion of its Western purchases through the development and sale of energy resources. But the bank amendment began the process that ultimately nullified a seven billion dollar Soviet arrangement with American companies to exploit jointly gas fields near Yakutsk that would have sent liquified natural gas to the U.S. and Japan.

Kissinger announced on 14 January 1975, that the U.S.S.R. had rejected the entire economic package—tariffs, credits, Lend-Lease debts—under discussion since 1972. Even though détente failed to meet Soviet expectations, the imperatives for expanded trade with America remained. Shortfalls in Soviet grain production reached disastrous levels in 1975, and resulted in a five-day buying spree, from 16 July to 21 July, that ended only after the U.S.S.R. had bought 345 million bushels of wheat, corn, and barley from Cargill, Continental, and Cook Industries, Inc. The purchases made with little warning, upset the U.S. market and prompted the Ford administration to impose a moratorium on future sales. The ban was lifted in October but only after the Soviets agreed to minimum and maximum limits, six to eight million metric tons, on annual purchases of American grain. The Soviet's procurement of American goods had occurred at a heavy price. Without hope for a lower tariff and hence more exports to redress the balance of trade, their hard-currency debt rose from $1.4 billion in 1970 to $18.1 billion in 1979.

Détente also failed to produce the political benefits sought by Americans. The U.S.'s search for a graceful exit from the Indochina conflict had been a motivating factor for cooperative relations with the Soviet Union. The U.S.S.R. did help arrange the January 1973 cease-fire in Vietnam and it reduced aid to Hanoi during the critical period of the American withdrawal. But the Russians either would not or could not prevent North Vietnam from launching an offensive that overwhelmed the South. The blighted hope for détente's effect in Vietnam was matched by American disillusionment with Soviet activity in Mozambique and Angola. Soviet and Cuban intervention in Africa so upset the Ford administration that in the spring of 1976 it declined to schedule another session of the Joint Commercial Commission and it postponed other bilateral meetings including talks with the Soviets on an oil agreement.[12]

LIGHTSWITCH DIPLOMACY: DÉTENTE AND ECONOMIC WARFARE

Jimmy Carter struggled unsuccessfully to formulate a coherent policy toward the Soviet Union. A prime reason for his failure was that he entered the White House at a time when the power of the presidency had been diluted by events associated with Vietnam and Watergate. His own inexperience in foreign relations only accentuated his problems. Finally, détente had eroded the Cold War consensus that had been the basis for the political and economic position of previous administrations. The President's closest advisers for international affairs reflected this divergence in American opinion. Secretary of State Cyrus Vance and other State Department members frequently advocated cooperation with the U.S.S.R.; while National Security Adviser Zbigniew Brzezinski and his National Security Council (NSC) staff generally urged a confrontational approach. The conflicting advice led to on-again, off-again relations with the Soviet Union that critics labeled, "lightswitch diplomacy."

Two events occurred in the spring of 1977 to set the tone for American-Soviet relations during Carter's tenure. First, Secretary Vance transmitted to the Soviets several proposals intended as a breakthrough for another SALT treaty. That the American initiative differed from the Ford-Brezhnev Vladivostok Accord and evolved from unknown personalities in a new administration raised more anxiety among Soviet leaders. They rejected the initiative on 30 March 1977, handing the President a damaging set-back in foreign affairs. Second, President Carter announced in April the results of a study conducted by the Central Intelligence Agency. The CIA report predicted the Soviet Union would enter the world market as a buyer, not seller, of petroleum products as early as 1985. The sensational prediction triggered a review of the American-Soviet strategic balance by the NSC staff. Its report, in turn, led the following August to Presidential Directive Number 18 on relations with the Soviet Union. Concerning economic matters, the directive concluded that the U.S. "must take advantage of its economic strength and technological superiority to encourage Soviet cooperation in resolving regional conflicts, reducing tensions, and achieving adequately verifiable arms control agreements."[13]

Since America's greatest weapon, food, had been partially disarmed by the 1975 Grain Agreement, the only economic tool left for prying political concessions out of the Soviet Union was the U.S.'s control over the export of high technology products. To protest the treatment of Soviet dissidents, the arrest of a U.S. businessman, and the trial of two American reporters in Moscow, Washington denied an export license for a Sperry Univac computer ordered by the Telegraph Agency of the Soviet Union (TASS) for use during the 1980 Summer Olympics. On 1 August 1978, the U.S. upped the ante by forbidding Soviet access to American technology for extracting and processing oil and gas. Dresser Industries, with the sale of a drill bit plant to the U.S.S.R., inadvertently became the classic example of the effects of "lightswitch diplomacy." Its export license was successively granted, suspended, reviewed, reaffirmed, and withdrawn in the space of two years.

Turning trade on and off for political reasons stirred controversy in both private and public sectors. Carter's program of reprisal garnered the applause of some labor unions, Jewish organizations, and human rights groups but it attracted the criticism of several business associations who objected to the costs involved. The U.S.S.R. concluded that the U.S. was an unreliable trading partner and the country of last resort for the supply of sophisticated goods. By 1980, the American share of the West's high technology sales to the U.S.S.R. plummeted to 3.7% and the real or potential harm to American producers aroused further dissension. Pro-trade advocates such as Commerce Secretary Juanita Kreps and Treasury Secretary Michael

Blumenthal found themselves in opposition to the views of Defense Department officials and the NSC staff. Kreps and Blumenthal shared the State Department's skepticism for the value of economic diplomacy.

Finally, individual government agencies were not immune to conflicting opinion over America's relations with the Soviet Union. The Department of Commerce housed not only the Office of Export Administration that licensed and restricted U.S. sales to the U.S.S.R. but also the Bureau of East-West Trade with its avowed purpose of promoting closer economic ties. Shortly before Carter imposed restrictions on Soviet purchases, he delivered an anti-inflation speech that called for a cabinet-level task force to increase federal incentives for American exports including the removal of unwarranted and unnecessary trade controls. The mixed signals from the White House and the divided nature of the bureaucracy meant that the executive branch exerted limited influence over the review of the 1969 Export Administration Act (EAA) that came up for renewal by Congress in the spring of 1979.

The revised EAA represented a victory for the nation's pro-trade interests. The legislation's premise was suggested by the 1976 Bucy Report, which noted that the Soviet Union really did not want Western goods as much as Western know-how to improve permanently her economic and strategic capabilities. It differentiated then between technology and equipment, and recommended strengthening the regulations governing the former while lessening the export restrictions on manufactured goods. The 1979 Act focused on controlling processes not products, especially the "critical technologies" e.g, microelectronics. The EAA embodied this notion in the form of the Militarily Critical Technologies List, a classified document generated and kept by the Defense Department.

To the benefit of American manufacturers, EAA minimized controls and facilitated the licensing of exports.

In conjunction with the successful negotiation of a second SALT treaty (not ratified), President Carter's signature on the bill in September 1979 heralded another era of understanding and cooperation between the superpowers. These signs of détente's revival, however, were toppled when Soviet troops moved into Afghanistan in December. Carter revealed his frustration with the Soviets on 4 January 1980, when he announced sanctions against the U.S.S.R. The government limited Aeroflot service to American shores and reduced Soviet fishing privileges in American waters; embargoed grain sales above the limits set by the 1975 Grain Agreement, cancelling a Soviet offer to buy 17 million metric tons of wheat and corn; urged Americans not to participate in the 1980 Moscow Olympics; and suspended all licensed exports to the U.S.S.R. pending an interagency review. Based on this review, Carter on 18 March denied the Soviets all high technology products.

These sanctions destroyed the pro-trade intent of EAA. It appeared that American-Soviet relations had come full circle in 1980 by returning to the anti-trade, Cold War posture of the Eisenhower administration. Soviet adventures in Afghanistan brought near-universal domestic condemnation that seemed in harmony with Carter's use of economic reprisals. However, Carter realized that the unity he had sought since 1977 had eluded him once again. Many farmers and their allies in Congress and the administration, including Vice President Walter Mondale, opposed the embargo on cereals, while the business community generally accepted strictures on technology transfers, but condemned export sanctions that violated the EAA. Experts on international relations remained divided over the effectiveness of trade as a tool of foreign policy. Thus President Carter built the foundation for the strident rhetoric employed by his Republican successor, but he had failed to convince significant actors in agriculture, government, and industry who were wedded to a policy of economic detente.[14]

NOTES

1. Quote from *Public Papers of the Presidents: John F. Kennedy, 1961* (Washington, DC: GPO, 1962), 26.

2. Quote from *New York Times*, 13 April 1962.

3. Gunnar Adler-Karlsson, *Western Economic Warfare, 1947-1967* (Stockholm: Almquist & Wiksell, 1968), 131; George W. Ball, *The Discipline of Power* (Boston: Little, Brown, 1968), 276; A. Paul Kubricht, "Politics and Foreign Policy: A Brief Look at the Kennedy Administration's Eastern European Diplomacy," *Diplomatic History* 11 (Winter 1987), 55-65.

4. Quote from *Congressional Record*, 88th Cong., 1st Sess., 1963, 21886.

5. *New York Times*, 8 November 1963; Rowland Evans and Robert Novack, *LBJ: The Exercise of Power* (New York: New American Library, 1966), 366; Dean Rusk, "The Battle Act Report, 1964," *Mutual Defense Assistance Control Act of 1951, Seventeenth Report to Congress* (Washington, DC: GPO, December 1964), 10; Arthur Schlesinger, *A Thousand Days: John F. Kennedy in the White House* (New York: Houghton Mifflin, 1965), 920.

6. Quote from *Report to the President of the Special Committee on U.S. Trade Relations* (Washington, DC: GPO, 1965), 10-11.

7. George C. Herring, *America's Longest War: The United States and Vietnam, 1950-1975* (New York: Wiley, 1979), 164-168; Libbey, "Soviet-American Trade," 198-199; *Public Papers of the Presidents: Lyndon B. Johnson, 1966*, 2 vols. (Washington, DC: GPO, 1967), 1128.

8. George D. Holliday, "Western Technology Transfer to the Soviet Automotive Industry," in Bruce Parrott, ed., *Trade, Technology, and Soviet-American Relations* (Bloomington: Indiana University Press, 1985), 82-116; Johnson, *Vantage Point*, 297-301 and 481-485.

9. Connie M. Friesen, *The Political Economy of East-West Trade* (New York: Praeger, 1976), 155-171; Gaddis, *Russia, the Soviet Union, and the United States*, 254-268; Holliday, "Western Technology Transfer to the Soviet Automotive Industry," 86-88; Joni Lovenduski and Jean Woodall, *Politics and Society in Eastern Europe* (Bloomington: Indiana University Press, 1987), 328.

10. As noted in Gary K. Bertsch, "American Politics and Trade with the USSR," in Bruce Parrott, ed., *Trade, Technology, and Soviet-American Relations* (Bloomington: Indiana University Press, 1985), 246.

11. *US-USSR Trade and Economic Council* (New York: Council, 1977), 1-40.

12. Bertsch, "American Politics and Trade with the USSR, 248-250; Friesen, *The Political Economy of East-West Trade*, 161-163; Herring, *America's Longest War*, 257-259; U.S. Department of State, "Secretary Kissinger's News Conference of January 14," *Department of State Bulletin*, 72 (3 February 1975). See also Paula Stern, *Water's Edge: Domestic Politics and the Making of American Foreign Policy* (Westport: Greenwood, 1979).

13. As noted in Samuel Huntington, "Trade, Technology and Leverage: Economic Diplomacy," *Foreign Policy* 32 (Fall 1978), 65.

14. *An Analysis of Export Control of U.S. Technology, A DOD Perspective: A Report of the Defense Science Board Task Force on Export of U.S. Technology - The "Bucy Report"* (Washington, DC: DOD, 1976), 1-39; Jimmy Carter, *Keeping Faith: Memoirs of a President* (New York: Bantam, 1982), 475-476; John Gordon Raley, "The Use of Economic Sanctions as a Political Weapon in U.S.-Soviet Relations." Ph.D. Diss., University of Massachusetts, 1986, 124-154. The Soviets had hoped for a different relationship. See A. I. Belchuk, ed., *Novy etap ekonomicheskogo sotrudnichestva SSSR s razvitymi kapitalisticheskimi stranami* (Moscow: IMEMO Nauka, 1978).

Chapter 6

ISSUES IN AMERICAN-SOVIET
ECONOMIC RELATIONS, THE 1980's

As in the period immediately following the Revolution in 1917, there was an apparent contradiction between the U.S. and the Soviet Union's shared economic activity and diplomatic ties in the 1980's. The intensity of American-Soviet hostility especially in the first half of the decade prompted some commentators to refer to the era as the Second Cold War; yet in 1984 the total trade turnover reached $3.8 billion, nearly matching détente's peak year for American-Soviet commerce. Grain, of course, accounted for this anomalous situation.

THE GRAIN CONTRADICTION

As the Republican candidate for president in 1980 Ronald Reagan vowed, if elected, to lift the partial grain embargo put in place by Jimmy Carter. Candidate Reagan's position was simply good politics. He chastised Carter for being ineffective since the embargo had not forced the U.S.S.R. to remove its troops from Afghanistan. Domestic politics played a major role in the Reagan administration's sale of American cereals, largely feed grains for livestock, to the Soviet Union. On 25 April 1981, President Reagan removed the embargo, permitting the Soviets to buy 5.9 million metric tons of grain above the limits set by the 1975 Grain Agreement.

In March 1981, the president had warned farmers that he might have to declare a total agricultural embargo though he promised not to do so unless it involved all goods and had the cooperation of America's allies. His commitment corresponded with the intent of the new Agricultural and Food Act (1981) which increased the compensation to farmers in the event of a government-imposed restriction on agricultural exports. Russian troops in Afghanistan, Soviet aid to Angola and Nicaragua, the Kremlin's complicity in the Polish Crisis, and the Soviet attack on KAL Flight 007 led President Reagan to describe the U.S.S.R. as "the evil empire;" yet his administration consistently sought to place American-Soviet agricultural trade on a sound commercial footing.

In 1981 and 1982 the Americans and Russians extended the original grain agreement on an annual basis. The following year the Reagan administration negotiated a long-term pact on grain that lasted until 1 October 1988. From the American side, it offered a high degree of stability in the export trade by forcing the Soviets, regardless of internal production, to buy nine million metric tons of grain annually of which eight million tons had to be divided equally between wheat and corn. From the Soviet side, the high minimum levels virtually eliminated the threat of another partial embargo. The new agreement also provided flexibility as the Soviets could substitute soybeans or soybean meal on a two for one basis for corn or wheat— which they did in 1986. And the U.S.S.R. had the option of buying an additional three million tons of coarse or fine grain.

For a variety of reasons, the U.S. government developed a vested interest in promoting the sale of grain or food-related products to the Soviet Union. It was militarily non-strategic; it represented one of the few bright spots in the nation's otherwise dark picture of trade deficits; it required the Russians to allocate hard-currency funds for non-technological goods; and it benefitted American farmers. When American-Soviet political relations shifted from rhetoric to negotiations in Reagan's second term of office, his administration targeted food and food processing equipment as the desired area for any commercial expansion. In the months preceding the 1986 Reykjavik Summit, the U.S. briefly offered to subsidize wheat sales to the U.S.S.R. under the Food Enhancement Program. The U.S. Department of Commerce beefed up its marketing section in the U.S. Commercial Office in Moscow and sponsored a major exhibit at a Soviet food fair, the first such U.S. exhibit in seven years.

While approving large grain sales, the Reagan administration employed vigorous measures (see below) to restrict globally the sale of manufactures to the Soviet Union. Western leaders and U.S. exporters sharply questioned and occasionally denounced the president's actions. Although the Reagan administration countered its critics by stating that industrial trade differed fundamentally from agricultural commerce, its grain policy undermined its other efforts to limit Western goods available for Soviet import. This inconsistency became even more pronounced when paired with the president's conviction that trade could be used to alter Soviet behavior. As long as the Soviets require huge grain imports, the four nations (U.S., Canada, Australia, and Argentina) with significant surpluses hold, especially in concert, considerable power. Since the U.S. has been reluctant to exercise this power, it appears that America's ideological differences with the Soviet Union cannot compete with domestic political and economic needs.[1]

TABLE 9

U.S.S.R. Grain Production and Imports, 1978-1988			
(In Millions of Metric Tons)			
Year	Grain Production	Grain Imports	Total	Imports as % of Total
1977/78	195.7	18.9	214.6	8.8
1978/79	237.4	15.6	253.0	6.1
1979/80	179.2	31.0	210.2	14.7
1980/81	189.1	34.8	223.9	15.5
1981/82	158.2	47.3	205.5	23.0
1982/83	186.8	34.3	221.1	15.5
1983/84	192.2	32.5	224.7	14.4
1984/85	172.6	55.5	228.1	24.3
1985/86	191.7	29.9	221.6	13.4
1986/87	210.1	28.5	238.6	11.9
1987/88*	211.3	32.0	243.3	13.1

*Projected

Adapted from: U.S. Department of Agriculture. "USSR Grain Situation and Outlook." FAS Circular (9 February 1988).

ECONOMIC DIPLOMACY

Trade with Russia has been a high-profile instrument of American diplomacy since the abrogation of the Commercial Treaty in 1911. Various administrations have employed commerce in the attempt to advance America's foreign policy objectives through cooperation with the Soviet Union. However, trade often has been used to chastise the Russians or force changes in the conduct of their government. The Reagan administration initially accepted the latter tradition of using commerce for coercion and retribution in its dealings with the Soviet Union. Sympathetic to the Cold War roots of American diplomacy and suspicious of all non-agricultural trade with the U.S.S.R., the president and his advisers found in the Polish Crisis an opportunity to punish the Soviets through restriction of commerce.

On 13 December 1981, the Polish Premier, General Wojciech Jaruzelski, declared martial law. It capped an 18-month period of internal unrest that began in July 1980 when the government announced huge increases in meat prices. The announcement set off a wave of strikes that spread in August to the key Baltic city of Gdansk. In order to reopen the critical port facilities and shipyards, the government acceded to 21 demands submitted by the workers. The government formally acknowledged the birth of a non-Communist union, soon called Solidarity, and affirmed its right to strike. This surrender to workers' demands resulted in a shake-up of government and party. The changes elevated General Jaruzelski, altered Poland from a party-state to an army-state and polarized government and worker. When Solidarity held its first (and last) national Congress in the fall of 1981, it behaved like an alternate political center; thus, martial law was directed primarily at destroying Solidarity by arresting its leaders.

The Reagan administration confirmed that Jaruzelski's actions occurred with Moscow's blessings and, favoring Solidarity's cause, exerted economic pressure on the Soviet Union in order to influence events in Poland. On 29 December 1981, the president proclaimed a long list of American sanctions. He suspended Aeroflot service, closed the Soviet Purchasing Commission (formerly, the Kama River Truck Plant Purchasing Commission), interrupted negotiations for a new maritime pact, postponed discussions for a long-term grain agreement, expanded the list of petroleum technology products that required a validated export license, suspended approvals for validated export licenses, and refused to renew exchange agreements on energy and technological cooperation. The next month, the U.S. gained NATO's endorsement for Reagan's preconditions for removing the sanctions: to lift martial law, to release detainees, and to resume the dialogue between Polish government and Solidarity. Finally, on 18 June 1982, over the strenuous objections by its allies the U.S. extended controls on oil and gas technology to American subsidiaries and licensees abroad.

Martial law ended in Poland a year after this last sanction went into effect. The U.S. government did have an impact on internal economic affairs through its simultaneous and direct application of punishments on Poland. However, no evidence emerged to suggest that American pressures on the Soviet Union forced changes or even moderated conditions in Poland. Indeed, the U.S. government implicitly acknowledged this fact when it began to dismantle the sanctions months before General Jaruzelski lifted martial law in July 1983.

Policy and leadership changes in the Soviet Union since 1983 contributed to the modification of America's use of economic diplomacy. The deaths of Brezhnev and two successors between 1982 and 1985 elevated several younger, more dynamic personalities to the Politburo headed by Mikhail S. Gorbachev. The U.S.S.R. announced in September 1986 an ambitious scheme to decentralize foreign commerce by giving 20 ministries and 70 enterprises the right to make deals directly with foreign partners including the formation of joint ventures with Western companies. Among other reforms, Gorbachev revived the idea of détente, suggesting it as a global model for the U.S.S.R. in a July 1986 speech. This activist phase in foreign affairs also included Soviet initiatives toward China. Meanwhile, in his second term, President Reagan sought to improve the opportunities for world peace through an arms control agreement with the Soviet Union.

This convergence of political purpose between Washington and Moscow found its corollary in economic relations. The two countries signed a ten-year extension to the Agreement on Economic, Industrial, and Technical

Cooperation. They also reconstituted the moribund U.S.-U.S.S.R. Commercial Commission, reopening the government-to-government trade dialogue in 1985. In 1986 and 1987, the U.S. government participated in commercial exhibits in the U.S.S.R. as the Soviet government inaugurated an advertising campaign for its products in America. Finally, as negotiations for a pact on intermediate range nuclear missiles reached a critical stage in August 1987, President Reagan announced his selection of C. William Verity, former Chairman of Armco Steel, to replace the late Malcolm Baldridge as Commerce Secretary. Armco had a 50-year history of involvement in Soviet trade, and Verity had served on the Board of Directors of the U.S.-U.S.S.R. Trade and Economic Council.

In terms of economic diplomacy the contrast between the 1981 Polish Crisis and the 1987 arms pact is instructive. As an instrument of coercion, commerce fell short of altering Soviet conduct toward Poland. Several reasons account for this failure. First, domestic needs and politics neutralized the nation's most serious economic weapon, grain. Second, the U.S. government neither calculated the domestic costs nor negotiated the full aproval of America's allies. Both factors reduced and diminished the effectiveness of the sanctions. Third, rather than seeking to moderate conditions through small but realistic steps, the U.S. attempted to force sweeping changes that it must have known were unacceptable to the Soviet Union. The Reagan administration successfully employed economic diplomacy as an adjunct to its quest for the December 1987 arms agreement. The measures adopted in this case, however, were as prudent as they were consistent. Not just the 1980s, but the full history of American-Soviet relations suggests that trade is not a potent tool for prying major political concessions from the U.S.S.R. It apparently works best in the limited though important role as a signal to mark America's pleasure or displeasure with Soviet behavior.[2]

THIRD-PARTY NATIONS

Third-party nations have helped to determine the structure, content, and amount of commerce exchanged by America and Russia since the eighteenth century. In the modern period, Anglo-Soviet accords led to the establishment of institutions facilitating the renewal of American-Russian trade in the early 1920s. The oscillations between friendship and enmity that characterized Russo-German relations in the 1930s had a direct impact on the quantity and type of goods shared by the U.S. and U.S.S.R. And the most dramatic illustration of this theme can be found in the Lend-Lease era. The significance of third-party nations continued in the postwar world, through blocs of nations rather than individual countries. For example, the Soviet Union initially directed most of its foreign trade activities toward Eastern Europe and created Comecon. Still, by the late 1980s, over half the Soviet Union's foreign trade (largely barter) was being conducted within the Comecon framework via 150 multilateral and more than 1,000 bilateral trade agreements.

The commitment to Comecon limits Soviet commerce with non-Socialist nations. Comecon's parallel organization in the West, the European Economic Community (EEC), has had a measurable bearing on American-Soviet trade. After the Marshall Plan and the initial CoCom embargo, Western Europe began to evade and then reject America's notion of using the West's economic strength as a means of political confrontation with the Soviet bloc. One element in this divergent approach is Western Europe's geographical proximity and cultural ties to the East. Another is that Comecon and the EEC have developed a complex set of economic relations tied to significant industrial interests. Finally, many Europeans linked the intensification of trade, industrial, and scientific cooperation that emerged in the 1970s with the hope for peace and prosperity. They valued economic interdependency as a means of raising the cost of military conflict.

Even though the U.S. had favored a similar policy toward Germany in the 1950s (i.e., integrate Germany's economy with Western Europe's to neutralize revisionist sentiment and avoid another war), it applied an entirely different set of principles toward the Soviet bloc. The attitude of the U.S. hovered somewhere between caution and opposition on the subject of Comecon's interaction with the EEC. For example, the U.S. has consistently argued that any West European reliance on Soviet energy could have dangerous economic, hence political and strategic repercussions in a future test of wills between East and West. The problem reappeared in the Eleventh Five-Year Plan (1980-1985) when Soviet decision-makers chose to develop natural gas reserves primarily from the Urengoi fields in Western Siberia. A major component in this development was the construction of five pipelines leading to European Russia plus an export line. This enormous transmission network required 20,000 kilometers of 56-inch pipe plus 230 compressor stations to move the gas.

The Soviets worked out credit or barter arrangements with West European governments and firms to exchange Soviet gas for Western pipe and compressors, especially for the export line. Allied participation in Soviet energy development disturbed the Reagan administration. At the Ottawa Economic Summit, 19-21 July 1981, the president urged the other leaders to reassess the Soviet project and to pursue alternative sources of natural gas. America's allies, though, indicated that they intended to proceed. Thwarted in its effort to mold an allied consensus, the U.S. government issued a warning directed at friend and foe alike. The Commerce Department disclosed that the administration was considering sanctions that would prohibit American subsidiaries and foreign companies from exporting U.S. licensed energy equipment and technology to the U.S.S.R., e.g., rotor parts for the turbines used in compressor stations.

The decision to apply these new sanctions was left in abeyance pending allied support for credit restrictions on East-West trade. This maneuver had two purposes. Soviet hard currency reserves might drop, interfering with the U.S.S.R.'s acquisition of sophisticated equipment from the West. And, by making credit more expensive, the pipeline project might be delayed while the U.S. sought alternatives for Europe's energy needs. The idea was flawed by the fact that EEC credit restrictions on Soviet trade had been abandoned two decades earlier. Nevertheless, at the Versailles Economic Summit of 5-6 June 1982, President Reagan proposed to limit credits and raise the costs of financing East-West commerce, however, the allies turned him down. On 18 June Reagan announced the extraterritorial extension of U.S. controls on energy-related products. His announcement angered the allies. The EEC lodged a formal protest on 14 July and threatened court action. Just in case the point was missed, the British and French approved laws that prohibited U.S. subsidiaries from complying with American sanctions.

The resulting turmoil provided ammunition for American critics of Reagan's policy. Under the leadership of the U.S. Chamber of Commerce, the business community censored the president for his "unprecedented blanket prohibition over U.S. subsidiaries and affiliates."[3] On 10 August, the House Foreign Affairs Committee voted 22-12 in approving a resolution that called on the President to abolish the latest sanctions. With the Western alliance in disarray and in the face of mounting pressure from business and Congress, the Reagan administration retreated. On 13 November 1982, Reagan announced he had ended extraterritorial controls because he had secured "substantial agreement" among the allies for a unified economic strategy. Within hours, the French government publicly dissociated itself from the announcement in Washington.

Eighteen months later the Reagan administration lifted the remaining controls on petroleum technologies and by 1987 Soviet representatives opened talks with an American firm for a joint venture to develop oil fields in the Arkhangel'sk region of the Soviet Arctic. And in November 1987 a Connecticut petroleum-engineering firm signed a U.S.-U.S.S.R. joint venture to develop control systems for oil refineries and petro-chemical plants. Obviously, third-party nations influenced the U.S. to adjust its position. The change occurred, however, without the U.S. government conceding that economic well-being is an integral part of security and that East-West trade contributes to the growth of the West's economy and hence to its strength. The U.S. government failed to acknowledge the inherent difficulties in an unilateral commercial policy toward the U.S.S.R., especially one based on limitations or restrictions. The interdependent nature of the world's economy and the widespread availability of substitutes subvert a policy of trade denial.[4]

TECHNOLOGY TRANSFER

Whether threshers, sewing machines, and typewriters in the 1890s or computers, fiber optics, and robotics in the 1980s, Americans have always held a comparative technological advantage over the Russians. This advantage has made America significant to the material progress of Russia. As early as the 1930s, the U.S. recognized this fact and exploited America's superiority as an element of economic diplomacy when it withheld aircraft and aviation fuel technology during the 1939-1941 "moral embargo." The Cold War era witnessed the establishment of the export licensing program that initially prevented the U.S.S.R. from acquiring even minimally processed goods. With the relaxation in controls in the 1960s, there was still a tendency to ban the export of not only military hardware but of articles that could play a dual, civilian-military role such as trucks. In the 1970s, technology transfer attracted greater attention until by the 1980s it became the premier issue in American-Soviet economic relations.

TABLE 10

U.S.-U.S.S.R. Low Technology Trade, 1981			
(in Millions of Dollars)			
A. Top 10 U.S. Exports to U.S.S.R.		**B. Top 10 U.S. Imports from U.S.S.R.**	
Commodity	*Value*	*Commodity*	*Value*
Corn	782	Fuel oil (light)	81
Wheat	773	Ammonia	78
Phosphoric acid	166	Palladium	31
Tracklaying tractors	57	Nickel	26
Tracklaying tractor parts	49	Naphtha	22
Tallow	49	Gold bullion	21
Tractor parts	35	Uranium fluorides	11
Petroleum coke	33	Fuel oil (heavy)	9
Copper ore	25	Sable furskins	8
Pipe handlers	24	Platinum group metals	6
Others	346	Others	54
Total	2,339	Total	347

Adapted from: Val Zabijaka. Unpublished Report. IEP/EUR/USSR Affairs Division, U.S. Department of Commerce (June 1982).

In the Reagan administration, concern for the strategic consequences of East-West trade was centered in the Defense Department. In 1981, it prepared a white paper, *Soviet Military Capabilities*, that included a discussion about the impact of American technology on Soviet military might. The white paper mirrored the opinions of Defense Secretary Caspar Weinberger and key members of his staff such as Richard Perle. Perle had served as Senator

Jackson's aide and point man for the Jackson-Vanik Amendment. In his new post, he became a vocal proponent for greater restrictions in American-Soviet commerce. The Reagan administration developed proposals designed to stem the flow of American and Western technology to the Soviet Union. The measures included increasing the efforts against industrial espionage, expanding the control list of militarily critical technologies, getting the U.S. academic community to reduce Soviet access to scholarly research, and strengthening American and allied (CoCom) export controls except for agricultural commodities and processes.

Some elements of the package went into effect almost immediately because they involved internal decisions that were relatively free of public discussion at home or abroad. For example, the Reagan administration placed a high priority on gathering intelligence, toughening enforcement, and prosecuting cases arising from the illicit traffic in military arms and advanced technology. The U.S. Customs Service began with extra funds from the Defense Department for a special project, Operation Exodus, to reduce the unlawful export of weaponry and equipment. At the same time, the Defense Department exercised its prerogatives under the 1979 EAA to enlarge the Militarily Critical Technologies List. The actual list was a classified document and safe from any conflicting pressure that might be exerted by American sellers and foreign buyers because public debate over the list's contents would constitute a breach of national security.

By February 1981, pronouncements from several sources revealed the administration's desire to increase the level of secrecy in American scientific research, not simply classified study, but general research conducted in many universities, published in scholarly journals, and presented at professional conferences. The presidents of several institutions including Cornell, MIT, and Stanford promptly informed Secretaries of Commmerce, Defense, and State of their opposition to any effort that would apply export restrictions to the academic community. While ideologically-motivated groups such as the Heritage Foundation and the Institute for Strategic Trade endorsed the administration's policy, more representative organizations such as the National Academy of Sciences cautioned in 1981 and again in 1987 that control and compartmentalization of basic research would impede scientific, economic, and military advances. The administration pursued its notion of secrecy via restrictions attached to government-funded research but it generally failed to acquire the academic community's support.

The problems that plagued the Reagan administration's approach to scientific research—wide-ranged and poorly-defined restrictions—reemerged in America's quest to secure an allied consensus on technology transfer. On the surface, the one forum best suited to the U.S. position was CoCom, the Paris-based, non-treaty organization composed of NATO countries plus Japan. Since 1949, CoCom had identified military hardware and technology that the several nations subsequently denied the Soviet Union. CoCom delegates met weekly in the 1980s to make decisions on exception requests for items on the embargo list and to review triennially the list itself. The U.S. strove to reassert America's leadership over its deliberations. At U.S. insistence, CoCom members agreed to increase the group's budget, modernize its office equipment, enlarge its staff, and expand its office space. Moreover, the U.S. successfully gained CoCom's endorsement to add Poland to the "no exceptions" policy established for the U.S.S.R. after the Soviet invasion of Afghanistan.

Finally, at America's urging, CoCom between 1982 and 1984, thoroughly reviewed embargoed items. The interim witnessed a U.S. effort to bend CoCom in the direction of America's position on the technology issue. It was an unproductive approach because the allies sharply distinguished between trade for economic benefits and trade denial for military reasons. CoCom's technically-oriented delegates preferred to downplay politics—contrary to America's emphasis—and only discuss export restrictions on those goods or technologies with an obvious bearing on the military capabilities of Communist nations. The U.S. rejected this narrow definition of strategic trade and submited a hundred proposals to expand CoCom's list.

It was not simply the number but the variety of recommendations that caused European and Japanese CoCom delegates to complain. The Departments of State and Defense sponsored different proposals and failed to present unified suggestions. Traditionally, the U.S. State Department took charge of discussions on export controls within the CoCom system. In the 1980s this responsibility was assigned to the Office of East-West Trade with its director, William A. Root. The Office of East-West Trade tried to improve CoCom in small steps that acknowledged the high value placed on Soviet and East European commerce by America's allies. The Defense Department argued that circumstances warranted a radically different approach. It advocated broadening and tightening export controls with the submission of a number of propositions to CoCom.

At first, the dispute over tactics between State and Defense was confined to an interagency coordinating group, the President's Export Council Subcommittee on Export Administration. These bureaucratic squabbles soon affected the Paris meetings of CoCom and finally splashed into the public arena. On 24 September 1983, Director Root resigned his post in protest. His open letter to the President and Congress revealed his frustration in trying to meet Defense Department demands for the application of stringent controls when CoCom members found such proposals abrasive. Root claimed that those who most wanted to strengthen strategic trade restrictions were doing the most to weaken them. Defense officials further strained the Western alliance by advocating the withdrawal of selected military technologies from friendly nations to force allied compliance.

The U.S. succeeded in stopping sales of communications equipment and creating a watch list of emerging technologies but it did not convince CoCom to ban computers and robotics. And even the successes soon faced challenges. In the fall of 1984, West Germany recommended an exception request for Standard Elektrik Lorenz, an American subsidiary of International Telephone and Telegraph Corporation. The German-based firm wanted to sell computerized telephone exchanges to Hungary. While American pressure quashed the request, it provided a startling illustration of the disparity in views between America and CoCom. Furthermore, CoCom failed to address what the Reagan administration had come to consider as a key problem in the technology area: how to prevent CoCom's neutral trading partners from shipping embargoed goods to Comecon nations.

Allied-American disputes in CoCom became even more disagreeable when the administration submitted several caustic proposals for the renewal of the Export Administration Act. The President and his advisers, heavily influenced by the Defense Department, sent to Congress a legislative agenda which, if approved, would have given the executive branch sweeping powers to use economic punishments against foreign violators of U.S. national security controls. While a significant number of senators sympathized with the President's position, House members responded to American and foreign business complaints by reducing the opportunities for applying economic diplomacy to friendly nations. Unable to agree on a new act, Congress twice extended EAA before allowing it to lapse at the end of February 1984. It forced the President to invoke the International Emergency Economic Powers Act to continue his authority to administer an export control policy until Congress

approved a compromise Export Adminstration Amend-
ments Act in 1985.

The setbacks at home and abroad prompted hard-line
officials to bypass Congress and CoCom and seek internal
sources of authority to advance their policy goals. For
example, the administration moved to end the transfer of
technology to the Soviet bloc via neutrals, targeting Austria
because of the country's heavy trade with both CoCom and
Comecon nations. In the latter half of 1984 the U.S.
applied economic diplomacy to Vienna by threatening to
withhold high technology goods from the Austrian market.
The tactic partly succeeded when the Austrians introduced
legislation in December 1984 that provided jail terms and
heavy fines for companies and individuals who violated the
terms of licenses issued by foreign governments for the
import of goods to Austria. But, reducing the flow of
technology through one neutral country failed to address
the larger problem, in fact, the Pentagon had already
encouraged the Commerce Department to devise
extraterritorial controls on the reexport of American
products.

The Department of Commerce, however, exhibited a
split personality on the technology transfer issue because of
its incompatible roles as promoter of American sales and
guardian of export controls. Commerce generally took the
position of the Defense Department during Reagan's first
term, in part because Defense officials had urged the
transfer of the export control function to the Customs
Service. The turf war among three agencies spurred the
Commerce Department to adopt a strident position on
technology transfer so as to preserve its jurisdiction over
the Export Control Administration. It doubled its budget
for the export control program, increased eight-fold the
number of export control officers, and in January 1984, it
bowed to Pentagon pressure by publishing preliminary
regulations designed to impede the reexport of American-
licensed products to unfriendly nations. The proposed rules

would have required foreign distributors to hand the U.S. government detailed quarterly reports on the individuals or firms buying American products. But when the new regulations finally went into effect 18 months later, 23 July 1985, they had been completely rewritten. Foreign distributors were asked to bar American goods from customers who did not supply end-use information. In short, the U.S. government screened foreign distributors and relied on their good will to prevent the diversion of high technology goods to America's adversaries.

The difference between the preliminary and final regulations was the result of an intensive debate. The U.S. business community felt the preliminary export measures would only confirm America's sour reputation in foreign trade and result in the U.S. relinquishing the lucrative high technology field to its many competitors world-wide. Accompanying the criticism of the proposed regulations were the monthly figures that showed a troublesome balance of trade as American exports failed by $100 billion annually to keep pace with imports. These two factors combined to persuade the Commerce Department to modify its program for extraterritorial trade restrictions. By the end of December 1984, Acting Assistant Commerce Secretary William T. Archey conceded that it was impossible to stop the transfer of technology while Undersecretary of Commerce for International Trade Lionel H. Olmer admitted that the export control list itself had become "bloated beyond all proportion."[5]

In 1985, Domestic and foreign events continued to sway the Commerce Department toward a flexible position on the technology transfer issue. As the U.S. crossed the line from creditor to debtor nation, the shock of America's dismal performance in world markets formed the backdrop to a debate over foreign trade by the White House and the Congress. The President found himself struggling to stave off the growing sentiment in Congress for protectionist legislation directed against America's allies, especially

Japan. Under these difficult circumstances the White House became amenable to adminstration pro-trade advocates, neutralizing the hard-line position of Defense officials. As a result, in March, the Commerce Department developed new rules on sales to the Soviet bloc: American products could be shipped to Communist countries if the exporter could prove that similar goods from other industrial nations were available in comparable quality and in such quantity that controlling them would no longer improve U.S. national security. Oddly, the mandate for the new foreign availability program had been established by the expired EAA of 1979. The program enabled the Soviet Union to buy from the U.S. a wide array of high technology products, such as personal computers and weather forecasting equipment.

President Reagan indirectly advanced the movement to modify export controls when he created the Commission on Industrial Competitiveness. By the spring of 1986, the Commission determined that the administration's export control policy had cost the U.S. 300,000 jobs and $12 billion annually in lost sales. The crisis over commerce was heightened by the realization in 1986 that for the first time in history the U.S. was posting a deficit even in high technology trade. The Commerce Department responded to the continuing furor over foreign trade by drafting regulations in June 1986 to streamline the licensing process. It established a pre-certification program that enabled approved exporters (and their customers) to trim weeks off the time required to secure a license for controlled products. And in March 1987, Commerce also eased controls over foreign-made products incorporating American-licensed components.

Thus the East-West technology trade issue gradually submerged into a sea of interrelated problems during the 1980s. Some of these problems were the controversy over the transfer of technology between West and West, the irreconcilable differences between America and CoCom allies in defining strategic trade, and the counterproductive shifts in U.S. policy from multilateralism to unilateralism. Other problems were the administrative style of President Reagan which permitted interagency rivalries to diminish a coherent policy, the disputes between the U.S. government and the academic community over the secrecy on scientific research, the concern of American business leaders that unwieldy export controls had virtually destroyed America's reputation as a reliable trading partner, and the awkward divisions within Congress which made the body ineffective in attempting to protect the American market and promote American sales abroad. Finally, there were the worries in national and international financial and governmental circles over America's unacceptably high trade deficits.

The juxtaposition of two cases that gained widespread notoriety in the summer of 1987 shed some light on the extraordinary complexities found in the East-West technology transfer issue. Brewing for more than six months, a scandal broke out in June with the disclosure that a subsidiary of Toshiba Corporation of Japan and the state-owned Kongsberg Vapenfabrikk of Norway had sold to the Soviet Union a number of computer-controlled milling machines between 1981 and 1984. The Soviets used them to manufacture state-of-the-art propellers for submarines and aircraft carriers. It was the most striking violation of CoCom export regulations since the group was founded in 1949. In Congress, the scandal served to bolster protectionist sentiment, but sanctions against Toshiba would cost an estimated 4,500 American jobs and against Kongsberg would disrupt the U.S. Navy's contract for the Penguin air-to-ship missile. While Congress considered legislation in mid-summer to ban Toshiba and Kongsberg products from American shores, the Commerce Department moved to approve the sale of IBM's Model 4381 mainframe computer system to Transnautic Shipping, a West German firm partly owned by the Soviet Union. The license would have been unthinkable a short time earlier and outside the context of the trade deficit that reached the staggering figure of $170 billion in 1986, including a $2.7 billion shortfall in high technology trade. Pentagon officials fought the approval in a year-long battle with the Commerce Department. The final twist to the story was that during the interim Transnautic had lost patience with both IBM and U.S. export controls and had bought a comparable mainframe computer system from one of IBM's foreign competitors, Hitachi.[6]

NOTES

1. Reinhard Rode, "The United States," in Reinhard Rode and Hanns-D. Jacobsen, eds., *Economic Warfare or Detente: An Assessment of East-West Relations in the 1980s* (Boulder, Co: Westview, 1985), 191-192; U.S. Congress, Joint Economic Committee, *East-West Commercial Policy: A Congressional Dialogue with the Reagan Administration* (Washington, DC: GPO, 1982); U.S. Department of Agriculture, "U.S./Soviet Grain," *FAS Fact Sheet* (2 Feb. 1987); Franklin J. Vargo, "U.S.-U.S.S.R. Trade Climate Improves, But Soviet Import Abilities Weakens," *Business America* 9 (21 July 1986), 6-8.

2. Boris Aristov, "Economic Changes Open Doors to Trade," *The Journal of Commerce* (8 Dec. 1986), 1, 2, & 32; Raymond L. Garthoff, *Detente and Confrontation: American-Soviet Relations from Nixon to Reagan* (Washington, DC: Brookings, 1985), 1033-1034; Andrzej Korbonski, "Poland," in Teresa Rakowska-Harmstone, ed., *Communism in Eastern Europe* (Bloomington: Indiana University Press, 1984), 57-62. See also Jadwiga Staniszkis, *Poland's Self-limiting Revolution* (Princeton, NJ: Princeton University Press, 1984).

3. Quote from *International Trade Reporter: U.S. Export Weekly* (16 Feb. 1982), 558.

4. "Glasnost Makes a Deal," *Time* (23 Nov. 1987), 57; Harald Muller, "U.S. Energy Policy," in Reinhard Rode and Hanns-D. Jacobsen, eds., *Economic Warfare or Detente: An Assessment of East-West Relations in the 1980s* (Boulder: Westview, 1985), 206-209; U.S. Congress, Joint Economic Committee, *The Soviet Economy in the 1980s: Problems and Prospects* (Washington, DC: GPO, 1982).

5. Quote from *New York Times*, 1 Jan. 1985. *New York Times*, 2 Jan.1985 and 27 Jan. 1985; Angela E. Stent, "East-West Economic Relations and the Western Alliance," in Bruce Parrott, ed., *Trade,*

Technology, and Soviet-American Relations (Bloomington: Indiana University Press, 1985), 310-316; U.S. Senate, *Reauthorization of the Export Administration Act* (Washington, DC: GPO, 1983); Stephen Woolcock, "East-West Trade: U.S. Policy Versus European Interests," *Soviet and Eastern European Foreign Trade* 19 (Spring 1983), 3-16. See also Gary K. Bertsch, *East-West Strategic Trade, COCOM and the Atlantic Alliance* (Paris: Atlantic Institute, 1983); National Academy of Sciences, *Scientific Communication and National Security*, 2 vols. (Washington, DC: National Academy, 1982).

6. *New York Times*, 15 Mar. 1985, 19 & 24 May 1985, 18 June 1986, 6, & 11 Dec. 1986, 16 Dec. 1986, 14 Jan. 1987, 9 Feb. 1987, 25 Mar. 1987; "Run Silent, Run to Moscow," *Time* (June 29, 1987), 45; "Shoot-Out at Tech Gap," *Time* (12 October 1987), 50-51.

Chapter 7

BIBLIOGRAPHY

GENERAL WORKS

Surveys are more interesting for their interpretations than for their descriptions of American-Russian/Soviet economic activity. World War II influenced Foster Dulles (entry 5) to view relations in terms of self-interest while the Cold War led Thomas Bailey (entry 3) into an anti-Soviet position. Pauline Tompkins (entry 13) challenged the notion of balance-of-power politics and William A. Williams (entry 15) presented an early and classic New Left criticism of American diplomacy. The best survey is by John Gaddis (entry 7) which employs a multi-faceted, systemic approach. Edited works, such as Eugene Anschel (entries 1 & 2) and Peter Filene (entry 6), collect samples of the love-hate relations between Americans and Russians, including business commentaries. Finally, there are a few works devoted exclusively to economic issues. Mikhail Condoide's (entry 4) pioneering monograph explores economic ties of the 1920s and 1930s. James Libbey (entry 11) outlined American-Soviet trade from 1917 to 1980 and Bruce Parrott (entry 12) edited an excellent series of articles that focus on Soviet technology problems and its trade with the U.S. during the last two decades. The unique work here is by Colin White (entry 14) who uses modeling theory and the comparative approach to explain the differences in the economic development of America and Russia.

1   Anschel, Eugene, ed. *American Appraisals of Soviet Russia, 1917-1977.* Metuchen, NJ: Scarecrow, 1978.

2   Anschel, Eugene, ed. *The American Image of Russia, 1775-1975.* New York: Ungar, 1974.

3   Bailey, Thomas A. *America Faces Russia: Russian-American Relations from early Times to our Day.* Ithaca, NY: Cornell University Press, 1950.

4   Condoide, Mikhail V. *Russian-American Trade: A Study of the Foreign-Trade Monopoly.* Columbus: Ohio State University Press, 1946.

5   Dulles, Foster Rhea. *The Road to Teheran: The Story of Russia and America, 1781-1943.* Princeton, NJ: University Press, 1944.

6   Filene, Peter G., ed. *American Views of Soviet Russia, 1917-1965.* Homewood, IL: Dorsey, 1968.

7   Gaddis, John Lewis. *Russia, the Soviet Union, and the United States: An Interpretive History.* New York: Wiley, 1978.

8   Garrison, Mary, and Abbott Gleason, eds. *Shared Destiny: Fifty Years of Soviet-American Relations.* Boston: Beacon, 1985.

9   Grayson, Benson L., ed. *The American Image of Russia, 1917-1977.* New York: Ungar, 1978.

10   Laserson, Max M. *The American Impact on Russia 1784-1917: Diplomatic and Ideological.* New York: Macmillan, 1950.

11   Libbey, James K. "Soviet-American Trade." In Joseph L. Wieczynski, ed. *The Modern Encyclopedia of Russian and Soviet History.* Vol. 36. Gulf Breeze, FL: Academic International, 1984, pp. 195-202.

12   Parrott, Bruce, ed. *Trade, Technology, and Soviet-American Relations.* Bloomington: Indiana University Press, 1985.

13   Tompkins, Pauline. *American-Russian Relations in the Far East.* New York: Macmillan, 1949.

14   White, Colin. *Russia and America: The Roots of Economic Divergence.* London: Croom Helm, 1987.

15   Williams, William Appleman. *American-Russian Relations, 1781-1947.* New York: Rinehart, 1952.

FROM AMERICAN TO RUSSIAN REVOLUTION

PERSONALITIES

Since Francis Dana's failures moved him to the rear of history's stage, few scholars are eager to revise W. P. Cresson's (entry 19) outdated and uncritical study. Frank Golder (entry 22) and David Griffiths (entry 23) note the foreign policy contradictions of Catherine II and her minister, Nikita Panin. John Quincy Adams (entry 16) played the more prominent role in American-Russian relations; see, Edward Crapol (entry 18), Howard Kushner (entry 46), Irby Nichols and Richard Ward (entry 47), Dexter Perkins (entry 48), and Patrick White (entry 41). Norman Saul (entries 27 & 28) biographically illustrates American entrepreneurial interest in Russia, though this involvement also led—see George Kennan (entry 24)—to negative appraisals of Tsarist Russia. American criticisms eventually coalesced around human rights issues resulting in the paradox of barren diplomacy and fruitful trade during World War I. See the memoirs of America's last ambassadors to the St. Petersburg Court: George Marye (entry 26) and David Francis (entry 21).

16 Adams, Charles F., ed. *John Quincy Adams in Russia, Comprising Portions of the Diary of John Quincy Adams from 1809 to 1814.* New York: Praeger, 1970.

17 Cockfield, Jamie H., ed. *Dollars and Diplomacy: Ambassador David Rowland Francis and the Fall of Tsarism, 1916-17.* Durham, NC: Duke University Press, 1981.

18 Crapol, Edward P. "John Quincy Adams and the Monroe Doctrine: Some New Evidence." *Pacific Historical Review* 48 (Aug. 1979), 413-418.

19 Cresson, W. P. *Francis Dana: A Puritan Diplomat at the Court of Catherine the Great.* New York: Dial, 1930.

20 Dvoichenko-Markov, Eufrosina. "Americans in the Crimean War." *Russian Review* 13 (Apr. 1954), 137-145.

21 Francis, David R. *Russia from the American Embassy: April 1916-November 1918.* New York: Scribner's, 1921.

22   Golder, Frank A. "Catherine II and the American Revolution." *American Historical Review* 21 (Oct. 1915), 92-96.

23   Griffiths, David M. "Nikita Panin, Russian Diplomacy, and the American Revolution." *Slavic Review* 28 (Mar. 1969), 1-24.

24   Kennan, George. *Siberia and the Exile System.* Abridged Reprint. Chicago: University of Chicago Press, 1958.

25   Loubat, Joseph Florimond. *Gustavus Fox's Mission to Russia, 1866.* New York: Arno, 1970.

26   Marye, George Thomas. *Nearing the End in Imperial Russia.* Philadelphia: Dorrance, 1979.

27   Saul, Norman [E.] "An American's Siberian Dream." *Russian Review* 37 (Oct. 1978), 405-420.

28   Saul, Norman [E.]"Beverley C. Sanders and the Expansion of American Trade with Russia, 1853-55." *Maryland Historical Magazine* 67 (Summer 1972), 156-171.

29   Saul, Norman [E.]"Jonathan Russell, *President Adams*, and Europe in 1810." *American Neptune* 30 (Oct. 1970), 279-290.

BEGINNINGS OF COMMERCE AND DIPLOMACY

Economic connections developed before the American Revolution. John Gaddis (entry 7) notes that Virginia tobacco found its way, via England, to Russian markets in the 17th century and Norman Saul (entry 36) points out that colonial merchants illegally opened direct trade with St. Petersburg in the 1760s. Commercial interests, then, influenced America's diplomatic efforts toward Russia; see especially W. P. Cresson (entry 19) and David Griffiths (entry 34). In a work filled with scholarship, grace, and humor, Alfred Crosby (entry 32) explores the importance of Russian naval stores for the Americans and U.S. shipping for the Russians during 1783-1812. The definitive generalized account of early relations is by Soviet scholar Nikolai Bolkhovitinov (entry 30) which supersedes an older study by John Hildt (entry 35).

30   Bolkhovitinov, Nikolai N. *The Beginnings of Russian-American Relations, 1775-1815.* Cambridge, MA: Harvard University Press, 1975.

31   Bolkhovitinov, Nikolai N. *Russia and the American Revolution.* Tallahassee, FL: Diplomatic Press, 1976.

32   Crosby, Alfred W. *America, Russia, Hemp, and Napoleon: American Trade with Russia and the Baltic, 1783-1812.* Columbus: Ohio State University Press, 1965.

33   Frederichson, J. William. "American Shipping in the Trade with Northern Europe, 1783-1880." *Scandinavian Economic History Review* 4 (1956), 110-125.

34   Griffiths, David M. "American Commercial Diplomacy in Russia, 1780-1783." *William and Mary Quarterly* 27 (July 1970), 379-410.

35   Hildt, John C. *Early Negotiations of the U.S. with Russia.* Baltimore, MD: Johns Hopkins University Press, 1906.

36   Saul, Norman E. "The Beginnings of American-Russian Trade, 1763-1766." *William and Mary Quarterly* 26 (Oct. 1969), 596-600.

37   Van Alstyne, Richard W. *Empire and Independence: The International History of the American Revolution.* New York: Wiley, 1965.

38   Trask, David F. and Sergei L. Tikhvinskii, eds. *The United States and Russia: The Beginning of Relations, 1765-1815.* Washington, DC: G.P.O., 1980.

39   Wharton, Francis, ed. *The Revolutionary Diplomatic Correspondence of the United States.* 6 vols. Washington, DC: G.P.O., 1889.

40   White, Patrick C. T. *A Nation on Trial: America and the War of 1812.* New York: Wiley, 1967.

RUSSIAN AMERICA

Russian America was the centerpiece in American-Russian relations from 1815 to 1867, see Benjamin Thomas (entry 49). Alexander I's restrictive ukase resulted in the 1824 Treaty and in a Russo-British agreement, see Irby Nichols and Richard Ward (entry 47). Dexter Perkins (entry 48) argues that the ukase prompted the noncolonization principle found in the Monroe Doctrine. Russia's colony in North America has many scholars; Hector Chevigny (entry 41) and Howard Kushner (entry 46) provide the best summaries. Readers interested in this subject should also consult such journals as *Oregon Historical Review, Pacific Historical Review, Russian Review, Slavic Review,* and

Washington Historical Quarterly. Ronald Jensen (entry 45) and Albert Woldman (entry 52) complement Chevigny and Kushner in detailing the sale of Russian America to the U.S. in 1867.

41   Chevigny, Hector. *Russian America: The Great Alaskan Venture, 1741-1867.* New York: Viking, 1965.

42   Dmytryshyn, Basil, and E. A. P. Crownhart-Vaughan, trans. and eds. *Colonial Russian America: Kyrill T. Khlebnikov's Reports, 1817-1832.* Portland: Oregon Historical Society, 1976.

43   Gibson, James R. *Imperial Russia in Frontier America: The Changing Geography of Supply of Russian America, 1784-1867.* New York: Oxford University Press, 1976.

44   Huculak, Mykhaylo. *When Russia Was in America: The Alaska Boundary Treaty Negotiations, 1824-25, and the Role of Pierre de Poletica.* Vancouver: Mitchell, 1971.

45   Jensen, Ronald J. *The Alaska Purchase and Russian-American Relations.* Seattle: University of Washington Press, 1975.

46   Kushner, Howard I. *Conflict on the Northwest Coast: American-Russian Rivalry in the Pacific Northwest, 1790-1867.* Westport, CT: Greenwood, 1975.

47   Nichols, Irby C., Jr., and Richard Ward. "Anglo-American Relations and the Russian Ukase: A Reassessment." *Pacific Historical Review* 41 (Nov. 1972), 444-459.

48   Perkins, Dexter. *A History of the Monroe Doctrine.* Boston: Little, Brown, 1963.

49   Thomas, Benjamin Platt. *Russo-American Relations, 1815-1867.* New York: Da Capo, 1970.

50   Tikhmenev, P. A. *A History of the Russian-American Company.* Seattle: University of Washington Press, 1978.

51   Wheeler, Mary E. "Empires in Conflict and Cooperation: The 'Bostonians' and the Russian-American Company." *Pacific Historical Review* 40 (Nov. 1971), 419-441.

52   Woldman, Albert A. *Lincoln and the Russians.* New York: Collier, 1961.

RUSSIAN ECONOMIC CONDITIONS

A comprehensive Western study of Russian economic conditions is by James Mavor (entry 61): while Soviet economic historian, Petr Liashchenko (entry 58), presents the Marxist-Leninist approach. The 1980s has witnessed a rebirth in the scholarship devoted to pre-Soviet economic history. Gregory Guroff and Fred Carstensen (entry 55) illustrate the diversity of Russian industrial communities while Alfred Rieber (entry 66) explores the sectoral competition among commercial groups. The chauvinism world view of Russian entrepreneurs is noted by Thomas Owen (entry 63) and Jo Ann Ruckman (entry 67). Foreign competition (John McKay, entry 60), bureaucratic obstacles (Thomas Owen, entry 64), and radical labor (Susan McCaffray, entry 59) led to pessimism among industrial managers and engineers before the fall of the Russian monarchy. For a discussion of American influence (Taylorism) on Russian industry, see Heather Hogan (entry 56) and Victoria King (entry 57).

53 Crisp, Olga. *Studies in the Russian Economy before 1914.* New York: Barnes & Noble, 1976.

54 Gatrell, Peter. *The Tsarist Economy 1850-1917.* New York: St. Martin's, 1986.

55 Guroff, Gregory, and Fred V. Carstensen, eds. *Entrepreneurship in Imperial Russia and the Soviet Union.* Princeton, NJ: Princeton University Press, 1983.

56 Hogan, Heather J. "Labor and Management in Conflict: The St. Petersburg Metal-Working Industry, 1900-1914." Ph.D. Diss., University of Michigan, 1981.

57 King, Victoria A. P. "The Emergence of the St. Petersburg Industrial Community, 1870-1905." Ph.D. Diss., University of California, 1982.

58 Liashchenko, Petr I. *History of the National Economy of Russia, to the 1917 Revolution.* New York: Macmillan, 1949.

59 McCaffray, Susan P. "The Association of Southern Coal and Steel Producers and the Problems of Industrial Progress in Tsarist Russia." *Slavic Review* 47 (Fall 1988), 464-482.

60 McKay, John P. *Pioneers for Profit: Foreign Entrepreneurship and Russian Industrialization, 1885-1913.* Chicago: University of Chicago Press, 1970.

61 Mavor, James. *An Economic History of Russia.* 2 vols. New York: Dutton, 1914.

62 Miller, Margaret. *The Economic Development of Russia, 1905-1914.* London: P. S. King, 1926.

6 3   Owen, Thomas C. *Capitalism and Politics in Russia: A Social History of the Moscow Merchants, 1855-1905.* Cambridge, Eng.: Cambridge University Press, 1981.

6 4   Owen, Thomas C. "The Russian Industrial Society and Tsarist Economic Policy, 1867-1905." *Journal of Economic History* 45 (Sept. 1985), 587-606.

6 5   Queen, George S. "American Relief in the Russian Famine of 1891-1892." *Russian Review* 14 (Apr. 1955), 140-150.

6 6   Rieber, Alfred. *Merchants and Entrepreneurs in Imperial Russia.* Chapel Hill: University of North Carolina Press, 1982.

6 7   Ruckman, Jo Ann. *The Moscow Business Elite: A Social and Cultural Portrait of Two Generations, 1840-1905.* DeKalb: Northern Illinois University, Press, 1984.

6 8   Robbins, Richard G., Jr. *Famine in Russia, 1891-1892: The Imperial Government Responds to a Crisis.* New York: Columbia University Press, 1975.

6 9   Von Laue, Theodore H. *Sergei Witte and the Industrialization of Russia.* New York: Columbia University Press, 1963.

U.S. SALES/INVESTMENTS

The scholarship on 19th century American-Russian economic relations is uneven and fragmented. Walther Kirchner (entry 79) examines American-Russian trade during the mid-19th century. Those interested in this topic might read Kirchner, George Queen (entry 84), and Gilbert Kohlenberg (entry 80) as a unit before moving on to specialty studies on Singer and/or International Harvester by Fred Carstensen (entry 70), Carstensen and Richard Werking (entry 71), and Elizabeth Pickering (entry 82). World War I's impact on diplomacy is discussed by Benson Grayson (entry 76) and on economics by Barbara Gaddis (entry 74). Jeanette Tuve (entry 85) suggests that, without the Russian Revolution, American capital would have extenuated the semi-colonial posture of Russia's economy.

7 0   Carstensen, Fred V. *American Enterprise in Foreign Markets: Studies of Singer and International Harvester in Imperial Russia.* Chapel Hill: University of North Carolina Press, 1984.

7 1   Carstensen, Fred V., and Richard Hume Werking. "International Harvester in Russia: The Washington-St.Petersburg Connection?" *Business History Review* 57 (Autumn 1983), 347-366.

7 2   Dowty, Alan. *The Limits of American Isolation: The United States and the Crimean War*. New York: New York University Press, 1971.

7 3   Fisher, Richard B. "American Investments in Pre-Soviet Russia." *American Slavic and East European Review* 8 (1949), 90-105.

7 4   Gaddis, Barbara Jackson. "American Economic Interests in Russia: August, 1914-March, 1917." M.A. Thesis, University of Texas, 1966.

7 5   Golder, Frank A. "Russian-American Relations During the Crimean War." *American Historical Review* 31 (Apr. 1926), 462-476.

7 6   Grayson, Benson Lee. *Russian-American Relations in World War I*. New York: Ungar, 1979.

7 7   Hogan, John V. "Russian-American Commercial Relations." *Political Science Quarterly* 27 (Dec. 1912), 631-647.

7 8   Kesaris, Paul, ed. *Confidential U.S. Diplomatic Post Records: Russia and the Soviet Union. Part 1: Russia: From Czar to Commissars, 1914-1918*. 10 reels. Frederick, MD: University Publications of America, 1982.

7 9   Kirchner, Walther. *Studies in Russian-American Commerce 1820-1860*. Leiden: Brill, 1975.

8 0   Kohlenberg, Gilbert Charles. "Russian-American Economic Relations, 1906-1917." Ph.D. Diss., University of Illinois, 1951.

8 1   Lewery, Leonard J. *Foreign Capital Investments in Russian Industries and Commerce*. Washington, DC: G.P.O., 1923.

8 2   Pickering, Elizabeth Cowan. "The International Harvester Company in Russia: A Case Study of a Foreign Corporation in Russia from the 1860s to the 1930s." Ph.D. Diss., Princeton University, 1974.

8 3   Queen, George S. "The McCormick Harvesting Machine Company in Russia." *Russian Review* 23 (Apr. 1964), 164-181.

8 4   Queen, George S. *The United States and the Material Advance in Russia, 1881-1906*. New York: Arno, 1976.

8 5   Tuve, Jeanette E. "Changing Directions in Russian-American Economic Relations, 1912-1917." *Slavic Review* 31 (Mar. 1972), 52-70.

AMERICAN-RUSSIAN FAR EASTERN RIVALRY

Russia's expansion into Manchuria and Korea challenged Japanese interests as well as the American policy of the Open

Door. Boris Romanov's (entry 89) authoritative work reflects access to Tsarist archives; see also Andrew Malozemoff (entry 87). Pauline Tompkins (entry 13) presents the American perspective, while John White (entry 92) notes that the U.S. welcomed "balanced antagonisms" (e.g., Russo-Japanese War) as a strategy for maintaining America's economic presence in the Far East. While Eugene Trani (entry 90) views the Treaty of Portsmouth as a stunning victory for President Theodore Roosevelt, Edward Zabriskie (entry 93) notes that U.S. dollar diplomacy suffered a setback in the subsequent Tokyo-St. Petersburg accord of 1912.

86   Dennett, Tyler. *Roosevelt and the Russo-Japanese War.* Gloucester, MA: P. Smith, 1959.

87   Malozemoff, Andrew. *Russian Far Eastern Policy 1881-1904; with Special Emphasis on the Causes of the Russo-Japanese War.* Berkeley: University of California Press, 1958.

88   Parsons, Edward B. "Roosevelt's Containment of the Russo-Japanese War." *Pacific Historical Review* 38 (Feb. 1969), 21-43.

89   Romanov, Boris A. *Russia in Manchuria, 1892-1906.* Ann Arbor, MI: J. W. Edwards, 1952.

90   Trani, Eugene P. *The Treaty of Portsmouth: An Adventure in American Diplomacy.* Lexington: University of Kentucky Press, 1969.

91   Walder, David. *The Short Victorious War: The Russo-Japanese Conflict, 1904-5.* New York: Harper & Row, 1973.

92   White, John Albert. *The Diplomacy of the Russo-Japanese War.* Princeton, NJ: Princeton University Press, 1964.

93   Zabriskie, Edward H. *American-Russian Rivalry in the Far East: A Study in Diplomacy and Power Politics, 1895-1914.* Philadelphia: University of Pennsylvania Press, 1946.

ABROGATION OF THE COMMERCIAL TREATY

Most of the two million Jews who fled Russia between 1880 and 1914 came to the U.S. As Ann Healy (entry 96) notes, Tsarist anti-Semitism so infringed upon U.S. citizens that the campaign against the treaty encountered little opposition even from American firms with Russian economic ties. Robert Maddox (entry 97) describes the origins and activities of the American Jewish Committee that sought to punish Russia by terminating the treaty. The debate and interaction between president and Congress over this issue is outlined by A. O. Sachs (entry 98).

9 4   Best, Gary Dean. *To Free a People: American Jewish Leaders and the Jewish Problem in Eastern Europe, 1890-1914.* Westport, CT: Greenwood, 1982.

9 5   Cohen, Naomi W. "The Abrogration of the Russo-American Treaty of 1832." *Jewish Social Studies* 25 (Jan. 1963), 3-41.

9 6   Healy, Ann E. "Tsarist Anti-Semitism and Russian-American Relations." *Slavic Review* 42 (Fall 1983), 408-425.

9 7   Maddox, Robert. "The American Jewish Committee and the Passport Question." M.A. Thesis, University of Wisconsin, 1958.

9 8   Sachs, A. O. "The Abrogation of the Russian American Treaty of 1832." M.A. Thesis, University of Wisconsin, 1947.

9 9   U.S. Congress, House Foreign Affairs Committee. *Termination of the Treaty between the United States and Russia.* Washington, DC: G.P.O., 1911.

RUSSIAN REVOLUTION TO WORLD WAR II

Joan Hoff-Wilson (entry 112) and Frederick Schuman (entry 117) observe the impact of ideology on American economic and political policy. Some commentators on the U.S.S.R. stress non-ideological factors; Ulam (entry 118) focuses on Soviet personalities and Russian traditions in foreign affairs while Uldrick (entry 119) underscores the pragmatic nature of Soviet foreign policy. Edward Bennett (entry 102), Donald Bishop (entry 103), and Robert Browder (entry 105) represent the standard of scholarship on the recognition issue. Thomas Maddux (entry 113) describes the 1930s as a period of estrangement in American-Soviet relations despite the Soviet drive for collective security against aggressor states.

100   Adams, Frederick C. *Economic Diplomacy: The Export-Import Bank and American Foreign Policy, 1934-1939.* Columbia: University of Missouri Press, 1976.

101   Batzler, Louis Richard. "The Development of Soviet Foreign Relations with the United States, 1917-1939." Ph.D. Diss., Georgetown University, 1956.

102   Bennett, Edward M. *Recognition of Russia: An American Foreign Policy Dilemma*. Waltham, MA: Blaisdell, 1970.

103   Bishop, Donald G. *The Roosevelt-Litvinov Agreements: The American View*. Syracuse, NY: Syracuse University Press, 1965.

104   Brandes, Joseph. *Herbert Hoover and Economic Diplomacy: Department of Commerce Policy, 1921-1928*. Pittsburgh, PA: University of Pittsburgh Press, 1962.

105   Browder, Robert Paul. *The Origins of Soviet-American Diplomacy*. Princeton, NJ: Princeton University Press, 1953.

106   Feis, Herbert. *The Diplomacy of the Dollar, 1919-1932*. Baltimore, MD: Johns Hopkins University Press, 1950.

107   Ferrell, Robert. *American Diplomacy in the Great Depression: Hoover-Stimson Foreign Policy, 1929-1933*. New Haven, CT: Yale University Press, 1957.

108   Filene, Peter G. *Americans and the Soviet Experiment, 1917-1933*. Cambridge, MA: Harvard University Press, 1967.

109   Gardner, Lloyd C. *Economic Aspects of New Deal Diplomacy*. Madison: University of Wisconsin Press, 1964.

110   Haslam, Jonathan. *Soviet Foreign Policy, 1930-33: The Impact of the Depression*. New York: St. Martin's, 1983.

111   Haslam, Jonathan. *The Soviet Union and the Struggle for Collective Security in Europe, 1933-39*. New York: St. Martin's, 1984.

112   Hoff-Wilson, Joan. Published under Wilson. *Ideology and Economics: U.S. Relations with the Soviet Union, 1918-1933*. Columbia: University of Missouri Press, 1974.

113   Maddux, Thomas R. *Years of Estrangement: American Relations with the Soviet Union, 1933-1941*. Tallahassee: University Press of Florida, 1980.

114   O'Connor, Timothy Edward. *Diplomacy and Revolution: G. V. Chicherin and Soviet Foreign Affairs, 1918-1930*. Ames: Iowa State University Press, 1988.

115   Parks, J. D. *Culture, Conflict and Coexistence: American-Soviet Cultural Relations, 1917-1958*. Jefferson, NC: McFarland, 1983.

116   Richman, John. *The United States and the Soviet Union: The Decision to Recognize*. Raleigh, NC: Camberleigh Hall, 1980.

117   Schuman, Frederick Lewis. *American Policy Toward Russia since 1917*. New York: International Publishers, 1928.

118   Ulam, Adam B. *Expansion and Coexistence: The History of Soviet Foreign Policy, 1917-67*. New York: Praeger, 1968.

119   Uldricks, Teddy J. *Diplomacy and Ideology: The Origins of Soviet Foreign Relations 1917-1930*. London: Sage, 1979.

PERSONALITIES

President Wilson's reaction to the Russian Revolution has been investigated by a small army of scholars. Betty Unterberger (entry 138) supplies a brief, thoughtful overview. Hammer, an American concessionaire has chronicled his business arrangements in his first autobiography (entry 129), a work also used to showcase and sell Russian art treasures. Philip Gillette (entry 128) gives a more balanced description of the same events. Floyd Fithian (entry 126) and Albert Parry (entry 137) note the farcical aspects to the concessions held by Sinclair and Vanderlip. In America, Gumberg and Nogin played key roles in reestablishing American-Russian trade, see James Libbey (entries 134 & 135). Beatrice Farnsworth (entry 125) records the disillu-sionment of Ambassador Bullitt. The autobiographical accounts of other ambassadors include: Joseph Davies (entry 124), and Averell Harriman and Elie Abel (entry 132). The best study on FDR and his relations with the Soviets is by Edward Bennett (entry 121).

120   Baer, George W., ed. *A Question of Trust: The Origins of U.S.-Soviet Diplomatic Relations: The Memoirs of Loy W. Henderson*. Stanford, CA: Hoover Institution, 1986.

121   Bennett, Edward M. *Franklin D. Roosevelt and the Search for Security: American-Soviet Relations, 1933-1939*. Wilmington, DE: Scholarly Resources, 1985.

122   Bland, Larry Irvin. "W. Averell Harriman: Businessman and Diplomat, 1891-1945." Ph.D. Diss., University of Wisconsin, 1972.

123   Considine, Bob. *The Remarkable Life of Dr. Armand Hammer*. New York: Harper & Row, 1975.

124   Davies, Joseph Edward. *Mission to Moscow*. New York: Simon & Schuster, 1941.

125   Farnsworth, Beatrice. *William C. Bullitt and the Soviet Union*. Bloomington: Indiana University Press, 1967.

126   Fithian, Floyd J. "Dollars Without the Flag: The Case of Sinclair and Sakhalin Oil." *Pacific Historical Review* 39 (May 1970), 205-222.

127   Gerberding, William P. "Franklin D. Roosevelt's Conception of the Soviet Union in World Politics." Ph.D. Diss., University of Chicago, 1959.

128   Gillette, Philip S. "Armand Hammer, Lenin, and the First American Concession in Soviet Russia." *Slavic Review* 40 (Fall 1981), 355-365.

129   Hammer, Armand. *The Quest of the Romanoff Treasure*. New York: William Farquhar Payson, 1932.

130   Hammer, Armand, with Neil Lyndon. *Hammer*. New York: Putnam, 1987.

131   Harriman, W. Averell. *America and Russia in a Changing World: Half a Century of Personal Observation*. Garden City, NY: Doubleday, 1971.

132   Harriman, W. Averell and Elie Abel. *Special Envoy to Churchill and Stalin, 1941-1946*. New York: Random House, 1975.

133   Levin, N. Gordon, Jr. *Woodrow Wilson and World Politics: America's Response to War and Revolution*. New York: Oxford University Press, 1968.

134   Libbey, James K. *Alexander Gumberg and Soviet-American Relations, 1917-1933*. Lexington: University Press of Kentucky, 1977.

135   Libbey, James K. "Nogin, Viktor Pavlovich (1878-1924)." In Joseph L Wieczynski, ed. *The Modern Encyclopedia of Russian and Soviet History*. Vol. 25. Gulf Breeze, FL: Academic International, 1981, pp. 43-45.

136   MacLean, Elizabeth Kimball. "Joseph E. Davies." Ph.D. Diss., University of Maryland, 1986.

137   Parry, Albert. "Washington B. Vanderlip, the 'Khan of Kamchatka.'" *Pacific Historical Review* 17 (Aug. 1948), 311-330.

138   Unterberger, Betty Miller. "Woodrow Wilson and the Bolsheviks: The 'Acid Test' of Soviet-American Relations." *Diplomatic History* 11 (Spring 1987), 71-90.

139 Walsh, William James. "Secretary of State Robert Lansing and the Russian Revolutions of 1917." Ph.D. Diss., Georgetown University, 1986.

AMERICA AND THE RUSSIAN REVOLUTION

George Kennan (entry 144) presents a well-written, definitive account of the Revolution. provoked in America. Christopher Lasch (entry 147) explores the differing views of opinionmakers and policymakers in America. The Bolshevik coup disappointed Ambassador Francis (entry 21), while the American Red Cross Commission worked with the Soviets, see Hermann Hagedorn (entry 142), William Hard (entry 143), and Libbey (entry 134). Albert Williams (entry 157) reminisces about the experiences he shared with other radical American journalists.

140 Foreign Policy Association. *Russian-American Relations, March, 1917-March, 1920*. New York: Harcourt, Brace & Howe, 1920.

141 Goldhurst, Richard. *The Midnight War: The American Intervention in Russia, 1918-1920*. New York: McGraw-Hill, 1978.

142 Hagedorn, Hermann. *The Magnate: William Boyce Thompson and His Time, 1869-1930*. New York: John Day, 1935.

143 Hard, William. *Raymond Robins' Own Story*. New York: Harper, 1920.

144 Kennan, George F. *Soviet-American Relations, 1917-1920*. 2 vols. New York: Atheneum, 1967.

145 Kettle, Michael. *The Allies and the Russian Collapse: March 1917-March 1918*. Minneapolis: University of Minnesota Press, 1981.

146 Killen, Linda. *The Russian Bureau: A Case Study in Wilsonian Diplomacy*. Lexington: University Press of Kentucky, 1983.

147 Lasch, Christopher. *The American Liberals and the Russian Revolution*. New York: Columbia University Press, 1962.

148 Sisson, Edgar G. *One Hundred Red Days: A Personal Chronicle of the Bolshevik Revolution*. New Haven, CT: Yale University Press, 1931.

149 Strakhovsky, Leonid Ivan. *The Origins of American Intervention in North Russia (1918)*. Princeton, NJ: Princeton University Press, 1937.

150   Unterberger, Betty Miller. *America's Siberian Expedition, 1918-1920: A Study of National Policy.* Durham, NC: Duke University Press, 1956.

151   Unterberger, Betty Miller, ed. *American Intervention in the Russian Civil War.* Boston: Heath, 1969.

152   U.S. Senate, Committee on Foreign Relations. *Relations with Russia.* Washington, DC: G.P.O., 1921.

153   U.S. Senate, Committee on Foreign Relations. *Russian Propaganda.* Washington, DC: G.P.O., 1920.

154   U.S. State Department. *Foreign Relations of the United States, 1918: Russia.* 3 vols. Washington, DC: G.P.O., 1931-32.

155   U.S. State Department. *Foreign Relations of the United States, 1919: Russia.* Washington, DC: G.P.O., 1937.

156   Warth, Robert D. *The Allies and the Russian Revolution: From the Fall of the Monarchy to the Peace of Brest-Litovsk.* Durham, NC: Duke University Press, 1954.

157   Williams, Albert Rhys. *Journey into Revolution: Petrograd, 1917-1918.* Chicago, IL: Quadrangle, 1969.

SOVIET ECONOMIC CONDITIONS

Alec Nove (entry 179) chronologically reveals the special features of the Soviet economy and supplants earlier works. The second volume of Edward Carr's (entry 166) detailed history of Soviet Russia is devoted to economic conditions from the Revolution to the NEP. Alexander Erlich (entry 170) illuminates the divergent policy recommendations favoring Soviet industrialization in the 1920s and Paul Haensel outlines the U.S.S.R.'s economic conditions on the eve of the First Five-Year Plan. Valerian Obolenskii and others (entry 180) provide an official report on Soviet planning while Boris Brutzkus (entry 165) and Naum Jasny (entry 177) provide a critical examination. John Littlepage (entry 179), a U.S. engineer employed by the Soviet Gold Trust, gives a first-hand account of the U.S.S.R.'s drive to industrialize.

158   Arnold, Arthur Z. *Banks, Credit, and Money in Soviet Russia.* New York: Columbia University Press, 1937.

159 Bailes, Kendall E. *Technology and Society Under Lenin and Stalin: Origins of the Soviet Technical Intelligentsia, 1917-1941.* Princeton, NJ: Princeton University Press, 1978.

160 Baykov, Alexander. *The Development of the Soviet Economic System.* New York: Macmillan, 1947.

161 Bergson, Abram. *The Real National Income of Soviet Russia Since 1928.* Cambridge, MA: Harvard University Press, 1961.

162 Bergson, Abram. *The Structure of Soviet Wages: A Study in Socialist Economics.* Cambridge, MA: Harvard University Press, 1944.

163 Bienstock, Gregory, Solomon M. Schwartz, and Aaron Yugow. *Management in Russian Industry and Agriculture.* New York: Oxford University Press, 1944.

164 Blackwell, William L. *The Idustrialization of Russia: An Historical Perspective.* New York: Crowell, 1970.

165 Brutzkus, Boris. *Economic Planning in Soviet Russia.* London: Routledge and Sons, 1935.

166 Carr, Edward Hallett. *A History of Soviet Russia. The Bolshevik Revolution, 1917-1923.* Vol. 2. New York: Macmillan, 1952.

167 Deutscher, Isaac. *Soviet Trade Unions: Their Place in Soviet Labour Policy.* London: Royal Institute of International Affairs, 1950.

168 Dewar, Margaret. *Labour Policy in the USSR, 1917-1928.* London: Royal Institute of International Affairs, 1956.

169 Dobb, Maurice H. *Soviet Economic Development since 1917.* London: Routledge & Kegan Paul, 1948.

170 Erlich, Alexander. *The Soviet Industrialization Debate, 1924-1928.* Cambridge: Harvard University Press, 1960.

171 Granick, David. *Management of the Industrial Firm in the USSR.* New York: Columbia University Press, 1954.

172 Haensel, Paul. *The Economic Policy of Soviet Russia.* London: King, 1930.

173 *Handbook of the Soviet Union.* New York: American-Russian Chamber of Commerce, 1936.

174 Hodgman, Donald R. *Soviet Industrial Production, 1928-1951.* Cambridge, MA: Harvard University Press, 1954.

175 Hubbard, Leonard E. *The Economics of Soviet Agriculture.* London: Macmillan, 1939.

176   Hunter, Holland. *Soviet Transportation Policy.* Cambridge, MA: Harvard University Press, 1954.

177   Jasny, Naum. *The Soviet Economy during the Plan Era.* Stanford, CA: Stanford University Press, 1951.

178   Littlepage, John D., and Demaree Bess. *In Search of Soviet Gold.* New York: Harcourt, Brace, 1938.

179   Nove, Alec. *An Economic History of the U.S.S.R.* Baltimore, MD: Penguin, 1969.

180   Obolenskii, Valerian V., and others. *Social Economic Planning in the USSR.* New York: International Industrial Relations Association, 1931.

181   Paslovsky, Leo, and Harold G. Moulton. *Russian Debts and Russian Reconstruction.* New York: McGraw-Hill, 1924.

182   Reddaway, William B. *The Russian Financial System.* London: Macmillan, 1935.

183   Timoshenko, Vladimir P. *Agricultural Russia and the Wheat Problem.* Stanford, CA: Food Research Institute and Hoover War Library, 1932.

184   Varga, Eugen. *Two Systems: Socialist Economy and Capitalist Economy.* New York: International Publishers, 1939.

THE SOVIET FOREIGN TRADE MONOPOLY

Alexander Baykov (entry 185) and Condoide (entry 4) represent the best of the early scholarship on the subject. Their efforts have been updated by John Quigley (entry 197) and Glen Smith (198). Smith includes an excellent description of the changes in foreign trade institutions, while Quigley outlines the origins and development of the monopoly before analyzing it functionally. James Libbey (entry 194) surveys the institutional predecessors to the current U.S.S.R. Chamber of Commerce. Soviet experts (entry 193) describe the legal foundations underlying the recent changes in Soviet foreign trade operations. Jerry Hough (entry 192) of Brookings discusses these changes from the American perspective.

185   Baykov, Alexander M. *Soviet Foreign Trade.* Princeton, NJ: Princeton University Press, 1946.

186   Boltho, Andrea. *Foreign Trade Criteria in Socialist Economies.* Cambridge, Eng.: Cambridge University Press, 1971.

187   Dohan, Michael Repplier. "Soviet Foreign Trade in the NEP Economy and Soviet Industrialization Strategy." Ph.D. Diss., Massachusetts Institute of Technology, 1970.

188   Gardner, H. Stephen. *Soviet Foreign Trade: The Decision Process.* Boston: Kluwer-Nijhoff, 1983.

189   Gruzinov, V. P. *The USSR's Management of Foreign Trade.* White Plains, NY: Sharpe, 1979.

190   Holzman, Franklyn D. *Foreign Trade Under Central Planning.* Cambridge, MA: Harvard University Press, 1974.

191   Holzman, Franklyn D. *International Trade Under Communism—Politics and Economics.* New York: Basic Books, 1976.

192   Hough, Jerry. *Opening Up the Soviet Economy.* Washington, DC: Brookings, 1988.

193   Levitsky, Serge L., ed. *The Reorganization of Soviet Foreign Trade: Legal Aspects.* Armonk, NY: Sharpe, 1989.

194   Libbey, James K. "Chamber of Commerce for the West." In Joseph L. Wieczynski, ed. *The Modern Encyclopedia of Russian and Soviet History.* Vol. 6. Gulf Breeze, FL: Academic International, 1978, pp. 197-199.

195   Liebowitz, Ronald D., ed. *Gorbachev's New Thinking: Prospects for Joint Ventures.* Cambridge, MA: Ballinger, 1988.

196   Patterson, Perry L. "Short-Run Forecasting and Planning for Soviet Foreign Trade with the West: An Econometric, Rational Expectations Approach." Ph.D. Diss., Northwestern University, 1986.

197   Quigley, John. *The Soviet Foreign Trade Monopoly: Institutions and Laws.* Columbus: Ohio State University Press, 1974.

198   Smith, Glen Alden. *Soviet Foreign Trade: Organization, Operations, and Policy, 1918-1971.* New York: Praeger, 1973.

199   Vajda, Imre, and Mihaly Simai, eds. *Foreign Trade in a Planned Economy.* Cambridge, Eng.: Cambridge University Press, 1971.

RUSSIAN FAMINE RELIEF

In addition to the official U.S. relief effort, Allen Wardwell directed the Russian Famine Fund and accepted the support of various groups that distrusted Secretary Hoover—see Libbey (entry 134) and Anne Meiburger (entry 204).

Earlier descriptions of the ARA, such as Harold Fisher's (entry 202), have been updated by Benjamin Weissman (entry 207) which is flawed somewhat by the author's excessive bias. For an intimate, first-hand account of the Soviet famine, see Frank Golder and Lincoln Hutchinson (entry 203).

200   Commission on Russian Relief. *The Russian Famines: 1921-22, 1922-23.* New York: National Information Bureau, 1923.

201   Eudin, Xenia J., and Harold H. Fisher, eds. *Soviet Russia and the West, 1920-1927.* Stanford, CA: Stanford University Press, 1957.

202   Fisher, Harold H. *The Famine in Soviet Russia, 1919-1923: The Operations of the American Relief Administration.* New York: Macmillan, 1927.

203   Golder, Frank A., and Lincoln Hutchinson. *On the Trail of the Russian Famine.* Stanford, CA: Stanford University Press, 1927.

204   Meiburger, Anne Vincent. *Efforts of Raymond Robins toward the Recognition of Soviet Russia and the Outlawry of War, 1917-1933.* Washington, DC: Catholic University of America Press, 1958.

205   Surface, Frank M., and Raymond L. Bland. *American Food in the World War and Reconstruction Period: Operations of the Organizations under the Direction of Herbert Hoover, 1914-1924.* Stanford, CA: Stanford University Press, 1931.

206   Wachhold, Allen Glen. "Frank A. Golder: An Adventure in Russian History." Ph.D. Diss., University of California, 1984.

207   Weissman, Benjamin M. *Herbert Hoover and Famine Relief to Soviet Russia: 1921-1923.* Stanford, CA: Hoover Institution Press, 1974.

208   Weissman, Benjamin M. "Herbert Hoover's 'Treaty' with Soviet Russia: August 20, 1921." *Slavic Review* 28 (June 1969), 276-288.

U.S. TRADE & BUSINESS INTERESTS IN THE U.S.S.R.

Philip Gillette (entries 220 and 221) and Libbey (entry 134) describe cotton's impact on the revival of trade. And James Libbey (entry 223) chronicles the resurrection of the American-Russian Chamber of Commerce.   American concessions are an interesting subject, see Floyd Fithian (entries 126 & 218), Bland (entry 122), Gillette (entry 128), Hammer (entry 129), and Parry (entry 137). Joan Hoff-Wilson (entry 222) suggests that U.S. business did not play a crucial role in the recognition episode, but commercial relations did create an foundation upon which diplomatic relations could be built. Lewis Feurer (entry 217), John McKay (entry 224), and Wladimir Naleszkiewicz (entry 225) summarize the influence of American technology and personnel on the Five-Year Plan. Antony Sutton (entries 228 & 229) provides a detailed account, but his analysis is marred by the claim that Soviet economic development depended almost entirely on Western technology.

209 Boe, Jonathan Evers. "American Business: The Response to the Soviet Union, 1933-1947." Ph.D. Diss., Stanford University, 1979.

210 Bron, Saul G. *Soviet Economic Development and American Business: Results of the First Year under the Five-Year Plan and Further Perspectives.* New York: H. Liveright, 1930.

211 Budish, Jacob M. *Soviet Foreign Trade: Menace or Promise.* New York: H. Liveright, 1931.

212 Clawson, Robert W., ed. "An American Businessman in the Soviet Union: The Reimer Report." *Business History Review* 50 (Summer 1976), 203-218.

213 Committee on Russian-American Relations. *The United States and the Soviet Union.* New York: American Foundation, 1933.

214 Dalrymple, Dana G. "American Technology and Soviet Agricultural Development, 1924-1933." *Agricultural History* 40 (July 1966), 187-206.

215 Dalrymple, Dana G. "The Stalingrad Tractor Plant in Early Soviet Planning." *Soviet Studies* 18 (Oct. 1966), 164-168.

216 *Economic Handbook of the Soviet Union.* New York: American-Russian Chamber of Commerce, 1931.

217 Feuer, Lewis S. "Travelers to the Soviet Union, 1917-1932: The Formation of a Component of New Deal Ideology." *American Quarterly* 14 (Summer 1962), 119-149.

218 Fithian, Floyd J. "American Business Participation in Russia, 1918-1933." Ph.D. Diss., University of Nebraska, 1964.

219   Friedman, Elisha Michael. *Russia in Transition: A Businessman's Appraisal.* New York: Viking, 1932.

220   Gillette, Philip S. "Conditions of American-Soviet Commerce: The Beginning of Direct Cotton Trade, 1923-1924." *Soviet Union* 1 (1974), 74-93.

221   Gillette, Philip S. "The Political Origins of American-Soviet Trade, 1917-1924." Ph.D. Diss., Harvard University, 1969.

222   Hoff-Wilson, Joan. Published under Wilson. "American Business and the Recognition of the Soviet Union." *Social Science Quarterly* 52 (Sept. 1971), 349-368.

223   Libbey, James K. "The American-Russian Chamber of Commerce." *Diplomatic History* 9 (Summer 1985), 233-248.

224   McKay, John P. "Foreign Enterprise in Russian and Soviet Industry: A Long-term Perspective." *Business History Review* 48 (Autumn 1974), 336-356.

225   Naleszkiewicz, Wladimir. "Technical Assistance of the American Enterprises to the Growth of the Soviet Union, 1929-1933." *Russian Review* 25 (Jan. 1966), 54-73.

226   Ropes, E. C. "American-Soviet Trade Relations." *Russian Review* 3 (Autumn 1943), 89-94.

227   Ropes, E. C. "The Shape of United States-Soviet Trade, Past and Future." *Slavic and East European Review* 3 (1944), 1-16.

228   Sutton, Antony C. *Western Technology and Soviet Economic Development 1917 to 1930.* Stanford, CA: Hoover Institution Press, 1968.

229   Sutton, Antony C. *Western Technology and Soviet Economic Development 1930 to 1945.* Stanford, CA: Hoover Institution Press, 1971.

230   Tereshtenko, Valery J. *American-Soviet Trade Relations: Past and Future.* New York: Russian Economic Institute, 1945.

231   Tuve, Jeanette Eckman. "Foreign Trade and Foreign Capital in the Development of the USSR to 1927." Ph.D. Diss., Case Western Reserve University, 1969.

232   U.S. Department of Commerce. *Trade of the United States with Union of Soviet Socialist Republics in 1939.* Washington, DC: G.P.O., 1940.

233   U.S. Department of Commerce. *Trade of the U.S. with the U.S.S.R.* Washington, DC: G.P.O., 1938.

234   U.S. Department of Commerce. *Trade of the U.S.S.R. with the United States in 1940.* Washington, DC: G.P.O., 1941.

LEND-LEASE

Lend-Lease is a well explored topic. Warren Kimball (entry 243) reveals its origins and Raymond Dawson (entry 236) explores Soviet participation. The best comprehensive studies are by George Herring (entry 239) and Robert Jones (entry 241). Edward Stettinius (entry 248) profiles the agency from his perspective as Lend-Lease Administrator, and U.S. State and War departments (entries 249 and 250) supply official statistics. Russian-born correspondent, Alexander Werth (entry 253), uses Soviet sources and personal observations to write a comprehensive study of the devastating war on the Eastern Front.

235 Carell, Paul. *Scorched Earth: The Russian-German War, 1943-1944*. Boston: Little, Brown, 1970.

236 Dawson, Raymond H. *The Decision to Aid Russia, 1941: Foreign Policy and Domestic Politics*. Chapel Hill: University of North Carolina Press, 1959.

237 Deane, John R. *The Strange Alliance: The Story of Our Efforts at Wartime Cooperation with Russia*. New York: Viking, 1947.

238 Fischer, Louis. *The Road to Yalta: Soviet Foreign Relations, 1941-1945*. New York: Harper & Row, 1972.

239 Herring, George C. *Aid to Russia: Strategy, Diplomacy, the Origins of the Cold War*. New York: Columbia University Press, 1973.

240 Jones, Jesse. *Fifty Billion Dollars: My Thirteen Years with the RFC, 1932-1945*. New York: Macmillan, 1951.

241 Jones, Robert Huhn. *The Roads to Russia: United States Lend-Lease to the Soviet Union*. Norman: University of Oklahoma Press, 1969.

242 Kerner, Robert J., ed. *USSR Economy and the War*. New York: Russian Economic Institute, 1943.

243 Kimball, Warren F. *The Most Unsordid Act: Lend-Lease, 1939-1941*. Baltimore, MD: Johns Hopkins University Press, 1969.

244 Langer, John Daniel. "The Formulation of American Aid Policy Toward the Soviet Union, 1940-1943: The Hopkins Shop and the Department of State." Ph.D. Diss., Yale University, 1975.

245   Levering, Ralph B. *American Opinion and the Russian Alliance, 1939-1945*. Chapel Hill: University of North Carolina Press, 1976.

246   Lukas, Richard C. *Eagles East: The Army Air Force and the Soviet Union, 1941-1945*. Tallahassee: Florida State University Press, 1970.

247   *Stalin's Correspondence with Churchill, Attlee, Roosevelt and Truman*. 2 vols. New York: Dutton, 1958.

248   Stettinius, Edward R. *Lend-Lease: Weapon for Victory*. New York: Macmillan, 1944.

249   U.S. State Department. *Report on War Aid Furnished by the United States to the U.S.S.R.* Washington, DC: G.P.O., 1945.

250   U.S. War Department. *International Aid Statistics, World War II*. Washington, DC: G.P.O., 1946.

251   Van Tuyll, Hubert Paul. "Lend-Lease and the Great Patriotic War, 1941-1945." Ph.D. Diss., Texas A&M University, 1986.

252   Voznesensky, Nikolai. *The Economy of the USSR During World War II*. Washington, DC: Public Affairs, 1948.

253   Werth, Alexander. *Russia at War, 1941-1945*. New York: Dutton, 1964.

AMERICAN-SOVIET ECONOMIC RELATIONS, 1945-88

GENERAL

Relations Since World War II

Walter LaFeber (entry 258) argues that the Cold War began in Europe but shifted toward newly-emerging nations in the mid-1950s, while Paul Hammond (entry 258) assumes that domestic political conditions influenced the way officials perceive and deal with foreign affairs. Adam Ulam (entry 263) contends that irrational premises and impulses underlie the policies of both nations, contributing to the danger posed by their superpower rivalry. While Lloyd Gardner (entry 256) also employs the power theme, Thomas Paterson (entry 261) suggests that this America's response led to the violation of its ideals of self-determination, democracy, and opportunity. See also surveys at the beginning of this bibliography, especially Gaddis (entry 7).

254 Caldwell, Dan. *American-Soviet Relations: From 1947 to the Nixon-Kissinger Grand Design*. Westport, CT: Greenwood, 1981.

255 Gaddis, John Lewis. *Strategies of Containment: A Critical Appraisal of Postwar American National Security Policy*. New York: Oxford University Press, 1982.

256 Gardner, Lloyd C. *A Covenant with Power: America and World Order from Wilson to Reagan*. New York: Oxford University Press, 1984.

257 Hammond, Paul Y. *Cold War and Detente: The American Foreign Policy Process*. New York: Harcourt, 1975.

258 LaFeber, Walter. *America, Russia, and the Cold War, 1945-1980*. New York: Wiley, 1980.

259 Levering, Ralph B. *The Cold War, 1945-1972*. Arlington Heights, IL: H. Davidson, 1982.

260 Nogee, Joseph L., and Robert H. Donaldson. *Soviet Foreign Policy since World War II*. New York: Pergamon, 1982.

261 Paterson, Thomas G. *Meeting the Communist Threat: Truman to Reagan*. New York: Oxford University Press, 1988.

262 Richmond, Yale. *U.S.-Soviet Cultural Exchanges, 1958-1986: Who Wins?* Boulder, CO: Westview, 1986.

263 Ulam, Adam B. *The Rivals: America and Russia Since World War II*. New York: Viking, 1971.

Origins of the Cold War

The causes of the Cold War have been endlessly debated. LaFeber (entry 258) notes U.S. economic motivation while Lynn Davis (entry 265) cites the Soviet abuse of self-determination in Eastern Europe. John Gaddis (entry 269) argues that Stalin had more options than the U.S. because the Soviet dictator was immune to the domestic pressures faced by American policymakers, and Daniel Yergin (entry 281) believes that the real Cold War culprit was America's fear of Soviet intentions. George Kennan (entry 274) is generally considered the philosophical father of the containment policy. Commentators and scholars have debated the containment policy's merits, a process in which Kennan himself has taken an active part (e.g., entry 273). Studies of Kennan's diplomacy can be found in Gaddis (entry 255) and Walter Hixson (entry 272).

264   Bailey, Thomas A. *The Marshall Plan Summer: An Eyewitness Report on Europe and the Russians in 1947.* Stanford, CA: Hoover Institution Press, 1977.

265   Davis, Lynn Etheridge. *The Cold War Begins: Soviet-American Conflict Over Eastern Europe.* Princeton, NJ: Princeton University Press, 1974.

266   DeSantis, Hugh. *The Diplomacy of Silence: The American Foreign Service, the Soviet Union, and the Cold War, 1933-1947.* Chicago: University of Chicago Press, 1980.

267   Douglas, Roy. *From War to Cold War, 1942-48.* New York: St. Martin's, 1981.

268   Etzold, Thomas H., and John Lewis Gaddis, eds. *Containment: Documents on American Policy and Strategy, 1945-1950.* New York: Columbia University Press, 1978.

269   Gaddis, John Lewis. *The United States and the Origins of the Cold War, 1941-1947.* New York: Columbia University Press, 1972.

270   Harrington, Virginia Marie. "The Quest for Consensus: U.S.-Soviet Relations, 1949-1952." Ph.D. Diss., Cornell University, 1987.

271   Henstridge, Steven Anthony. "The United States, the Soviet Union, and the North Atlantic Treaty, 1948-1949." Ph.D. Diss., Kent State University, 1986.

272   Hixson, Walter Lawrence. "From Containment to Neo-Isolation: The Diplomacy of George F. Kennan, 1944-1957." Ph.D. Diss., University of Colorado, 1986.

273   Kennan, George F. "George F. Kennan Replies." *Slavic Review* 35 (Mar. 1976), 32-36.

274   Kennan, George F. [Mr. X]. "The Sources of Soviet Conduct." *Foreign Affairs* 25 (July 1947), 566-582.

275   Mark, Eduard. "American Policy toward Eastern Europe and the Origins of the Cold War, 1941-1946: An Alternative Interpretation." *Journal of American History* 68 (Sept. 1981), 313-336.

276   Mastny, Vojtech. *Russia's Road to the Cold War: Diplomacy, Warfare, and the Politics of Communism.* New York: Columbia University Press, 1979.

277   Rose, Lisle A. *After Yalta.* New York: Scribner's, 1973.

278   Ryan, Henry Butterfield. *The Vision of Anglo-America: The US-UK Alliance and the Emerging Cold War 1943-1946.* Cambridge, Eng.: Cambridge University Press, 1987.

279   Siracusa, Joseph M., ed. *The American Diplomatic Revolution: A Documentary History of the Cold War, 1941-1947.* Port Washington, NY: Kennikat, 1977.

280   Wright, C. Ben. "Mr. 'X' and Containment." *Slavic Review* 35 (Mar. 1976), 1-31.

281   Yergin, Daniel. *Shattered Peace: The Origins of the Cold War and the National Security State.* Boston: Houghton Mifflin, 1977.

Detente's Rise and Fall

Gaddis (entry 7) summarizes the events leading to detente, see also Paul Herman (entry 288). Third World confrontations (John Armstrong, entry 282) chipped away at the initial optimism, as did the Jackson-Vanik Amendment (Paula Stern, entry 298). Even the Soviets, who more consistently supported detente than Americans, became worried by the human rights issue (Morton Schwartz, entry 296). Thomas Larson (entry 291) questioned whether commerce can be used for political leverage. Connie Friesen (entry 286) concluded that U.S. hopes were unrealistic, while other works tend to exhibit a strong interpretative bias. For example, Richard Pipes (entry 293) considers the Soviets to be belligerent and unyielding, while Richard Barnet (entry 283) criticizes the officialdom Pipes represents. See also Adam Ulam's (entry 301) "realistic" appraisal of Soviet foreign policy during the detente era.

282   Armstrong, John A. "Soviet-American Confrontation: A New Phase?" *Survey* 97 (Autumn 1975), 40-51.

283   Barnet, Richard J. *The Giants: Russia and America.* New York: Simon & Schuster, 1977.

284   Brafman, Morris, and David Schimel. *Trade for Freedom: Detente, Trade, and Soviet Jews.* New York: Shengold, 1975.

285   Edmonds, Robin. *Soviet Foreign Policy, 1962-1973: The Paradox of Super Power.* London: Oxford University Press, 1975.

286   Friesen, Connie M. *The Political Economy of East-West Trade.* New York: Praeger, 1976.

287   Gati, Charles, and Toby Trister Gati. *The Debate over Detente.* New York: Foreign Policy Association, 1977.

288   Herman, Paul Frank, Jr. "The Conceptualization and Conduct of U.S.-Soviet Detente." Ph.D. Diss., University of Pittsburgh, 1984.

289   Hoyt, Ronald E. *Winners and Losers in East-West Trade: A Behavioral Analysis of U.S.-Soviet Detente (1970-1980).* New York: Praeger, 1983.

290   Hulett, Louisa Sue. *Decade of Detente: Shifting Definitions and Denouement.* Washington, DC: University Press of America, 1982.

291   Larson, Thomas B. *Soviet-American Rivalry.* New York: Norton, 1978.

292   Neal, Fred Warner, ed. *Detente or Debacle: Common Sense in U.S.-Soviet Relations.* New York: Norton, 1979.

293   Pipes, Richard. *U.S.-Soviet Relations in the Era of Detente.* Boulder, CO: Westview, 1981.

294   Potichnyj, Peter J., and Jane P. Shapiro, eds. *From the Cold War to Detente.* New York: Praeger, 1976.

295   Rapoport, Anatol. *The Big Two: Soviet-American Perceptions of Foreign Policy.* New York: Pegasus, 1971.

296   Schwartz, Morton. *Soviet Perceptions of the United States.* Berkeley: University of California, 1978.

297   Sheldon, Della W., ed. *Dimensions of Detente.* New York: Praeger, 1978.

298   Stern, Paula. *Water's Edge: Domestic Politics and the Making of American Foreign Policy.* Westport, CT: Greenwood, 1979.

299   Stevenson, Richard W. *The Rise and Fall of Detente: Relaxations of Tensions in U.S.-Soviet Relations, 1953-84.* Urbana: University of Illinois, 1985.

300   Szulc, Tad. *The Illusion of Peace: Foreign Policy in the Nixon Years.* New York: Viking, 1978.

301   Ulam, Adam B. *Dangerous Relations: The Soviet Union in World Politics, 1970-1982.* New York: Oxford University Press, 1983.

Cooperation and Conflict in the 1980s

Raymond Garthoff (entry 304) details the ups and downs in American-Soviet ties, concluding that there is no serious alternative to detente and arms control. Joseph Nye's (entry 311) argues that the American system is subject to such varying pressures that U.S. foreign policy is untidy at best. Participants in a Hoover Institution conference (Richard Staar, entry 313), argues America tends to respond to Soviet actions rather than to explain U.S. society and policy. Alexander George's volume (entry 305) explores the difficulties involved in crisis prevention; while the same theme is obliquely supported in Robert German's (entry 306) work. Richard Staar (entry 314) assumes that every Soviet move is designed to facilitate world dominance, while Peter Savigear (entry 312) argues that the U.S. and U.S.S.R. are indistinguishable, have lost their moral credibility and are incapable of effectively meeting new global challenges

302 Caldwell, Dan, ed. *Soviet International Behavior and U.S. Policy Options.* Lexington, MA: Lexington Books, 1985.

303 Caldwell, Lawrence T., and William Diebold, Jr. *Soviet-American Relations in the 1980s: Superpower Politics and East-West Trade.* New York: McGraw-Hill, 1980.

304 Garthoff, Raymond L. *Detente and Confrontation: American-Soviet Relations from Nixon to Reagan.* Washington, DC: Brookings, 1985.

305 George, Alexander L., ed. *Managing U.S.-Soviet Rivalry.* Boulder, CO: Westview, 1983.

306 German, Robert K., ed. *The Future of U.S.-U.S.S.R. Relations: Lessons from Forty Years without World War.* Austin: University of Texas, 1987.

307 Heyns, Terry L. *American and Soviet Relations since Detente: The Framework.* Washington, DC: G.P.O., 1987.

308 Hyland, William. *Mortal Rivals: Superpower Relations from Nixon to Reagan.* New York: Random House, 1987.

309 Liska, George. *Rethinking US-Soviet Relations.* New York: B. Blackwell, 1987.

310   Lynch, Allen, and Kerry S. McNamara, eds. *Changing Dimensions of East-West Relations.* Boulder, CO: Westview, 1987.

311   Nye, Joseph S., Jr., ed. *The Making of America's Soviet Policy.* New Haven, CT: Yale University Press, 1984.

312   Savigear, Peter. *Cold War or Detente in the 1980s: The International Politics of American-Soviet Relations.* New York: St. Martin's, 1987.

313   Staar, Richard F., ed. *Public Diplomacy: USA Versus USSR.* Stanford, CA: Hoover Institution Press, 1986.

314   Staar, Richard F. *USSR Foreign Policies After Detente.* Stanford, CA: Hoover Institution Press, 1985.

PERSONALITIES

Political personalities have determined the course of American-Soviet economic relations while U.S. businessmen have played secondary roles. A biographer of U.S. entrepreneurs, Joseph Finder (entry 320) argues against American-Soviet trade expansion. William Taubman (entry 334) believes detente is an old Stalinist instrument of Soviet policy, and Fraser Harbutt (entry 323) suggests that Churchill was a key figure in the origins of the Cold War. Henry Walton (entry 335) reprieves Henry Wallace who was fired as Commerce Secretary in 1946 for criticizing President Truman's "get tough" policy with the Soviets. Important architects of the postwar order were Dean Acheson (entry 315) and George Kennan (entry 325). In addition to Kennan, the diplomatic service possessed several brilliant experts (e.g., Charles Bohlen, entry 317) who tried to educate American policymakers on the complexities of Russian communism.

315   Acheson, Dean. *Present at the Creation: My Years in the State Department.* New York: Norton, 1969.

316   Beam, Jacob. *Multiple Exposure: An American Ambassador's Unique Perspective on East-West Issues.* New York: Norton, 1978.

317   Bohlen, Charles E. *Witness to History.* New York: Norton, 1973.

318 Brezhnev, Leonid. *Peace, Detente, and Soviet-American Relations: A Collection of Public Statements.* New York: Harcourt, Brace Jovanovich, 1979.

319 Druks, Herbert. *Harry S. Truman and the Russians, 1945-1953.* New York: Speller, 1966.

320 Finder, Joseph. *Red Carpet: The Connection Between the Kremlin and America's Most Powerful Businessmen—Armand Hammer, Averell Harriman, Cyrus Eaton, David Rockefeller, Donald Kendall.* New York: Holt, Rinehart & Winston, 1983.

321 Goold-Adams, Richard. *The Time of Power: A Reappraisal of John Foster Dulles.* London: McLelland, 1962.

322 Gromyko, Anatolii. *Through Russian Eyes: President Kennedy's 1036 Days.* Washington, DC: International Library, 1973.

323 Harbutt, Fraser J. *The Iron Curtain: Churchill, America, and the Origins of the Cold War.* New York: Oxford University Press, 1986.

324 Kalb, Marvin, and Bernard Kalb. *Kissinger.* Boston: Little, Brown, 1974.

325 Kennan, George F. *Memoirs: 1925-1950.* Boston: Little, Brown, 1967.

326 Khrushchev, Nikita S. *Khrushchev in America: Full Texts of the Speeches Made by N. S. Khrushchev on His Tour of the United States, September 15-27, 1959.* New York: Crosscurrents, 1960.

327 McSherry, James E. *Khrushchev and Kennedy in Retrospect.* Palo Alto, CA: Open-Door, 1971.

328 Mandelbaum, Michael, and Strobe Talbott. *Reagan and Gorbachev.* New York: Vintage, 1987.

329 Messer, Robert L. *The End of an Alliance: James F. Byrnes, Roosevelt, Truman, and the Origins of the Cold War.* Chapel Hill: University of North Carolina Press, 1982.

330 Pribytkov, Victor, ed. *Soviet-U.S. Relations: The Selected Writings and Speeches of Konstantine U. Chernenko.* New York: Praeger, 1984.

331 Ruddy, Michael. *The Cautious Diplomat: Charles E. Bohlen and the Soviet Union, 1929-1969.* Kent, OH: Kent State University Press, 1986.

332 Smith, Walter Bedell. *My Three Years in Moscow.* Philadelphia: J. B. Lippincott, 1950.

333 Talbott, Strobe. *The Russians and Reagan.* New York: Vintage, 1984.

334   Taubman, William. *Stalin's American Policy: From Entente to Detente to Cold War.* New York: Norton, 1982.

335   Walton, Henry J. *Henry Wallace, Harry Truman and the Cold War.* New York: Viking, 1976.

THE SOVIET ECONOMY AND FOREIGN TRADE

Abram Bergson (entry 337), Stanley Cohn (entry 342), Harry Schwartz (entry 355), Nove (entry 179), and the popular account by Marshall Goldman (entry 346) contain useful background information. Ivan Evenko (entry 344) describes Soviet economic planning and Hans Hirsch (entry 348) analyzes the dual guidance system (physical/financial) used by planners to communicate objectives to Soviet enterprise managers. Robert Campbell (entry 341) notes that accounting information plays a more crucial role in Soviet than capitalist management. Fyodor Kushnirsky (entry 351) studies the methodology used by Soviet planners to gauge economic progress, while Bruce Parrott (entry 354) claims that the U.S.S.R. has lost the race between Soviet and Western economies. The Gorbachev leadership recognized this fact and began restructuring the economy. A thoughtful and detailed study of these reforms is by Ed Hewett (entry 347). The foreign trade monopoly is dealt with in an earlier section of this bibliography.

336   Arnot, Bob. *Controlling Soviet Labor: Experimental Change from Brezhnev to Gorbachev.* Armonk, NY: M. E. Sharpe, 1988.

337   Bergson, Abram. *Economic Trends in the Soviet Union.* Cambridge: Harvard University Press, 1963.

338   Bergson, Abram. *Productivity and the Social System-The USSR and the West.* Cambridge, MA: Harvard University Press, 1978.

339   Berliner, Joseph S. *Factory and Manager in the USSR.* Cambridge, MA: Harvard University Press, 1957.

340   Bialer, Seweryn, and Michael Mandelbaum, eds. *Gorbachev's Russia and American Foreign Policy.* Boulder, CO: Westview, 1988.

341   Campbell, Robert W. *Accounting in Soviet Planning and Management.* Cambridge, MA: Harvard University Press, 1963.

342 Cohn, Stanley H. *Economic Development in the Soviet Union.* Lexington, MA: Heath, 1970.

343 Dyker, David A. *The Future of the Soviet Economic Planning System.* Armonk, NY: M. E. Sharpe, 1985.

344 Evenko, Ivan A. *Planning in the USSR.* Moscow: Foreign Languages Publishing House, 1963.

345 Goldman, Marshall I. *Gorbachev's Challenge: Economic Reform in the Age of High Technology.* New York: Norton, 1987.

346 Goldman, Marshall I. *The Soviet Economy: Myth and Reality.* Englewood Cliffs, NJ: Prentice-Hall, 1968.

347 Hewett, Ed A. *Reforming the Soviet Economy: Equality versus Efficiency.* Washington, DC: Brookings, 1988.

348 Hirsch, Hans. *Quantity Planning and Price Planning in the Soviet Union.* Philadelphia: University of Pennsylvania Press, 1961.

349 Hoffman, Erik P., and Robbin F. Laird. *Technocratic Socialism: The Soviet Union in the Advanced Industrial Era.* Durham, NC: Duke University Press, 1985.

350 Ioffe, Olimpiad S., and Peter B. Maggs. *The Soviet Economic System: A Legal Analysis.* Boulder, CO: Westview, 1987.

351 Kushnirsky, Fyodor I. *Growth and Inflation in the Soviet Economy.* Boulder, CO: Westview, 1988.

352 Lane, David. *Soviet Labour and the Ethic of Communism: Full Employment and the Labour Process in the USSR.* Boulder, CO: Westview, 1987.

353 Linz, Susan J., and William Moskoff, eds. *Reorganization and Reform in the Soviet Economy.* Armonk, NY: M. E. Sharpe, 1988.

354 Parrott, Bruce. *Politics and Technology in the Soviet Union.* Cambridge, MA: MIT Press, 1983.

355 Schwartz, Harry. *Russia's Soviet Economy.* New York: Prentice-Hall, 1956.

356 Thomas, John R., and Ursula M. Kruse-Vaucienne, eds. *Soviet Science and Technology: Domestic and Foreign Perspectives.* Washington, DC: National Science Foundation, 1977.

357 U.S. Congress, Joint Economic Committee. *Soviet Economic Prospects for the Seventies.* Washington, DC: G.P.O., 1973.

358 U.S. Congress, Joint Economic Committee. *The Soviet Economy in the 1980s: Problems and Prospects.* Washington, DC: G.P.O., 1982.

359   ZumBrunnen, Craig, and Jeffrey P. Osleeb. *The Soviet Iron and Steel Industry.* Totowa, NJ: Rowman & Allanheld, 1986.

Agriculture

The Soviet need for grain has been the basis for American-Soviet economic relations. Shortfalls in Soviet agriculture (Robert Deutsch, entry 360) have been exacerbated by a revolution in consumer food demand, however, the crux of the issue is collectivization's failure, see Zhores Medvedev (entry 366). Efforts to improve production, such as Khrushchev's virgin lands policy, created as many problems as solutions, see Richard Mills (entry 367) and Alec Nove (entry 368). Werner Hahn (entry 361) and Erich Strauss (entry 369) reveal varied approaches of Soviet officialdom to this troubled economic sector. Since the late 1960s, agro-industrial integration became the cornerstone of Soviet policy according to Valentin Litvin (entry 365). The Brooks study within Johnson and Brooks (entry 362) indicates that American and Canadian grain output is double that of the U.S.S.R. and that the main difference is Soviet labor productivity which is lower by a factor of 10 or more. Thus systemic reforms, such as the incentive team program recommended by Gorbachev, are vital to improving performance.

360   Deutsch, Robert. *The Food Revolution in the Soviet Union and Eastern Europe.* Boulder, CO: Westview, 1986.

361   Hahn, Werner G. *The Politics of Soviet Agriculture, 1960-1970.* Baltimore, MD: Johns Hopkins University Press, 1972.

362   Johnson, D. Gale, and Karen McConnell Brooks. *Prospects for Soviet Agriculture in the 1980's.* Bloomington: Indiana University Press, 1983.

363   Jones, James R., ed. *East-West Agricultural Trade.* Boulder, CO: Westview, 1986.

364   Laird, Roy D., ed. *Soviet Agricultural and Peasant Affairs.* Lawrence: University of Kansas Press, 1963.

365   Litvin, Valentin. *The Soviet Agro-Industrial Complex: Structure and Performance.* Boulder, CO: Westview, 1987.

366   Medvedev, Zhores. *Soviet Agriculture.* New York: Norton, 1987.

367 Mills, Richard M. "The Formation of the Virgin Lands Policy." *Slavic Review* 29 (Mar. 1970), 58-69.

368 Nove, Alec. "Soviet Agriculture under Brezhnev." *Slavic Review* 29 (Sept. 1970), 379-410.

369 Strauss, Erich. *Soviet Agriculture in Perspective: A Study of its Successes and Failures.* New York: Praeger, 1969.

370 Walker, Martin. *The Waking Giant: Gorbachev's Russia.* New York: Pantheon, 1986.

Soviet Energy and the West

Books by Robert Campbell (entry 371 & entry 373) evaluate Russian capabilities and intentions for exporting petroleum. See also Robert Ebel (entry 376), a text that includes translations of Soviet commentaries on oil. Edward Friedland, et al. (entry 377) contends that oil is power and that the U.S.S.R. became the power winner of the 1970s, while other appraisals by Ed Hewett (entry 380) and Arthur Klinghoffer (entry 384) argue that oil politics play only a modest role in Soviet foreign policy. Hewett and George Hoffman (entry 381) note that Soviet petroleum products have clearly made Eastern Europe and Cuba more dependent on Russia. Marshall Goldman (entry 378) suggests that the CIA's mystifying assessments of Soviet reserves (entry 374) of 1977 was political wish-fulfillment. More recent estimates correctly show the enormous size of Soviet reserves; see Stephen Lewarne (entry 386) and Alexei Mahmoudov (entry 387).

371 Campbell, Robert W. *The Economics of Soviet Oil and Gas.* Baltimore, MD: Johns Hopkins University Press, 1968.

372 Campbell, Robert W. *Soviet Energy Technologies: Planning, Policy, Research and Development.* Bloomington: Indiana University Press, 1980.

373 Campbell, Robert W. *Trends in the Soviet Oil and Gas Industry.* Baltimore, MD: Johns Hopkins University Press, 1976.

374 Central Intelligence Agency. *The International Energy Situation.* Washington, D.C.: G.P.O., 1977.

375   *East-West Trade: An Analysis of Trade between Western Nations and the Soviet Bloc.* New York: American Management Association, 1964.

376   Ebel, Robert E. *Communist Trade in Oil and Gas: An Evaluation of the Future Export Capability of the Soviet Bloc.* New York: Praeger, 1970.

377   Friedland, Edward, Paul Seabury, and Aaron Wildavsky. *The Great Detente Disaster: Oil and the Decline of American Foreign Policy.* New York: Basic Books, 1975.

378   Goldman, Marshall I. *The Enigma of Soviet Petroleum: Half-Full or Half-Empty?* London: Allen & Unwin, 1980.

379   Hardt, John P., ed. *Tariff, Legal and Credit Constraints on East-West Commercial Relations.* Ottawa: Carleton University, 1975.

380   Hewett, Ed A. *Energy Economics and Foreign Policy in the Soviet Union.* Washington, DC: Brookings, 1984.

381   Hoffman, George W. *The European Energy Challenge: East and West.* Durham, NC: Duke University Press, 1985.

382   Jentleson, Bruce W. *Pipeline Politics: The Complex Political Economy of East-West Energy Trade.* Ithaca, NY: Cornell University Press, 1986.

383   Kapstein, Ethan Barnaby. "American Strategy and Alliance Energy Security, 1945-1980." Ph.D. Diss., Fletcher School of Law and Diplomacy, 1986.

384   Klinghoffer, Arthur Jay. *The Soviet Union and International Oil Politics.* New York: Columbia University Press, 1977.

385   Kosnik, Joseph T. *Natural Gas Imports from the Soviet Union: Financing the North Star Joint Venture Project.* New York: Praeger, 1975.

386   Lewarne, Stephen. *Soviet Oil: The Move Offshore.* Boulder, CO: Westview, 1988.

387   Mahmoudov, Alexei. *The Soviet Oil and Natural Gas Industries (Problems of Reserve Estimation).* Falls Church, VA: Delphic Associates, 1986.

388   Marer, Paul, ed. *US Financing of East-West Trade: The Political Economy of Government Credits and the National Interest.* Bloomington: Indiana University Press, 1975.

389   Mikesell, Raymond F., and Jack N. Behrman. *Financing Free World Trade with the Sino-Soviet Bloc.* Princeton, NJ: Princeton University Press, 1958.

390   Muller, Harald. "U.S. Energy Policy." In Reinhard Rode and Hanns-D. Jacobsen, eds. *Economic Warfare or Detente: An Assessment of East-West Relations in the 1980s.* Boulder, CO: Westview, 1985, pp. 200-212.

391   Sawyer, Herbert L. *Soviet Perceptions of the Oil Factor in U.S. Foreign Policy: The Middle East-Gulf Region.* Boulder, CO: Westview, 1983.

392   Sokoloff, George. *The Economy of Detente: The Soviet Union and Western Capital.* New York: St. Martin's, 1987.

393   Stein, Jonathan B. *The Soviet Bloc, Energy, and Western Security.* Lexington, MA: Lexington Books, 1983.

394   U.S. Library of Congress, Legislative Reference Service. *Soviet Oil in the Cold War.* Washington, DC: G.P.O., 1961.

Comecon

Margaret Dewar (entry 401) documents the reorientation of Eastern Europe's trade with the Soviet Union following World War II. The work by Jozef Brabant (entry 397) is an extensive account of Comecon's origin and development; see also Franklyn Holzman (entry 405) and Henry Schaefer (entry 410). James Libbey (entry 406) briefly surveys Comecon's evolution and principal issues involved in its development. Paul Marer has undertaken the difficult task of standardizing and interpreting Comecon's trade statistics. The Vienna Institute for Comparative Economic Studies (entry 412) periodically issues a compendium of Comecon data. Gerhard Fink's edited work (entry 403), also a product of the Vienna Institute, surveys the most important studies being conducted on economic reform in Eastern Europe.

395   Bornstein, Morris, Zvi Gitelman, and William Zimmerman, eds. *East-West Relations and the Future of Eastern Europe: Politics and Economics.* London: Allen & Unwin, 1981.

396   Brabant, Jozef M. van. *Essays on Planning, Trade and Integration in Eastern Europe.* Rotterdam: Rotterdam University Press, 1974.

397   Brabant, Jozef M. van. *Socialist Economic Integration: Aspects of Contemporary Economic Problems in Eastern Europe.* Cambridge, Eng.: Cambridge University Press, 1980.

398   Brada, Josef C., and V. S. Somanath, eds. *East-West Trade: Theory and Evidence*. Bloomington: International Development Institute of Indiana University, 1978.

399   Carnovale, Marco, and William C. Potter, eds. *Continuity and Change in Soviet-East European Relations: Implications for the West*. Boulder, CO: Westview, 1988.

400   Central Intelligence Agency. *Foreign Trade of the East European Communist Countries, 1960-1970: A Statistical Summary*. Washington, DC: G.P.O., 1972.

401   Dewar, Margaret. *Soviet Trade with Eastern Europe, 1945-1949*. London: Royal Institute of International Affairs, 1951.

402   Directorate of Economic Affairs. *Comecon: Progress and Prospects*. Brussels: NATO, 1977.

403   Fink, Gerhard, ed. *Economic Reform in Eastern Europe: Structural Problems, Investment Policy, and East-West Relations*. Boulder, CO: Westview, 1988.

404   Garrett, Stephen A. *From Potsdam to Poland: American Policy Toward Eastern Europe*. New York: Praeger, 1986.

405   Holzman, Franklyn D. *The Economics of Soviet Bloc Trade and Finance*. Boulder, CO: Westview, 1987.

406   Libbey, James K. "Comecon." In Joseph L. Wieczynski, ed. *The Modern Encyclopedia of Russian and Soviet History*. Vol. 47. Gulf Breeze, FL: Academic International, 1988, pp. 208-212.

407   Marer, Paul. "East European Economies: Achievements, Problems, Prospects." In Teresa Rakowska-Harmstone, ed. *Communism in Eastern Europe*. Bloomington: Indiana University Press, 1984, pp. 283-328.

408   Marer, Paul. *Soviet and East European Foreign Trade, 1946-1969: Statistical Compendium and Guide*. Bloomington: Indiana University Press, 1972.

409   Marer, Paul, and John Michael Montias, eds. *East European Integration and East-West Trade*. Bloomington: Indiana University Press, 1980.

410   Schaefer, Henry Wilcox. *Comecon and the Politics of Integration*. New York: Praeger, 1972.

411   U.S. Congress, Joint Economic Committee. *Economic Developments in the Countries of Eastern Europe*. Washington, DC: G.P.O., 1970.

412   Vienna Institute for Comparative Economic Studies. *Comecon Data 1987*. Westport, CT: Greenwood, 1988.

413 Wallace, William V., and Roger A. Clarke. *Comecon, Trade and the West.* New York: St. Martin's, 1986.

414 Wilczynski, Josef. *Technology in Comecon: Acceleration of Technological Progress Through Economic Planning and the Market.* New York: Praeger, 1974.

THE U.S. AND SOVIET TRADE

Aborted Aid to the U.S.S.R.

Herring (entry 239) and Jones (entry 241) contain information on the sour end to Lend-Lease; also see Gaddis (entry 7), Thomas Paterson (entry 420), and Herring (entry 416). Neither revisionists (e.g., Paterson, entry 418) nor orthodox (e.g., Leon Martel, entry 417) historians accept the Truman administration's claim that it "lost" the Soviet loan request. Lloyd Gardner (entry 415) concludes that the unsatisfactory loan episode was one of the principal features shaping the Cold War.

415 Gardner, Lloyd C. *Architects of Illusion: Men and Ideas in American Foreign Policy 1941-1949.* Chicago: Quadrangle Books, 1970.

416 Herring, George C. "Lend-Lease to Russia and the Origins of the Cold War, 1944-1945." *Journal of American History* 56 (June 1969), 93-114.

417 Martel, Leon. *Lend-Lease, Loans, and the Coming of the Cold War: A Study of the Implementation of Foreign Policy.* Boulder, CO: Westview, 1979.

418 Paterson, Thomas G. "The Abortive American Loan to Russia and the Origins of the Cold War, 1943-1946." *Journal of American History* 56 (June 1969), 70-92.

419 Paterson, Thomas G. *On Every Front: The Making of the Cold War.* New York: Norton, 1979.

420 Paterson, Thomas G. *Soviet-American Confrontation: Postwar Reconstruction and the Origins of the Cold War.* Baltimore, MD: Johns Hopkins University Press, 1973.

U.S. Trade Controls & the Western Embargo

Paterson (entry 420) highlights the formation of U.S. trade controls; see also Philip Green (entry 425) and Robert

Pollard (entry 430). When Gunnar Adler-Karlsson's (entry 421) book on the Western embargo appeared in 1968, his European colleagues had never heard of the embargo. CoCom began as a U.S.-sponsored gentlemen's agreement, a secret group with informal rules. European governments with strong Communist parties were reluctant to admit openly to an American-directed, anti-Soviet trade policy. Western businessmen knew of the embargo, but not the general public. After 1953, CoCom was no longer a secret organization though only brief and indirect references to its activities appeared in the European press. David Folts (entry 426) focuses on the conflicts and agreements that arose between president and Congress in their effort to fashion a strategic economic policy toward the Soviet Union; see also Suchati Chuthasmit (entry 423), Theodore Osgood (entry 427), and Ronald Salem (entry 431).

421   Adler-Karlsson, Gunnar. *Western Economic Warfare, 1947-1967.* Stockholm: Almqvist and Wiksell, 1968.

422   Berman, Harold J. "Thinking Ahead: East-West Trade." *Harvard Business Review* 32 (Sept./Oct. 1954), 147-158.

423   Chuthasmit, Suchati. "The Experience of the United States and Its Allies in Controlling Trade with the Red Bloc: 1948-1960." Ph.D. Diss., Fletcher School of Law and Diplomacy, 1961.

424   Edwards, Lee. "Congress and the Origins of the Cold War, 1946-1948." Ph.D. Diss., Catholic University of America, 1986.

425   Green, Philip Earl. "Conflict over Trade Ideologies During the Early Cold War: A Study of American Foreign Economic Policy." Ph.D. Diss., Duke University, 1978.

426   Folts, David William. "The Role of the President and Congress in the Formation of United States Economic Policy Towards the Soviet Union, 1947-1968." Ph.D. Diss., University of Notre Dame, 1971.

427   Osgood, Theodore K. "East-West Trade Controls and Economic Warfare." Ph.D. Diss., Yale University, 1957.

428   Pastor, Robert A. *Congress and the Politics of U.S. Foreign Economic Policy, 1929-1976.* Berkeley: University of California Press, 1980.

429 Pisar, Samuel. *A New Look at Trade Policy toward the Communist Bloc: The Elements of a Common Strategy for the West.* Washington, DC: G.P.O., 1961.

430 Pollard, Robert Allen. "Economic Security and the Origins of the Cold War: The Strategic Ends of U.S. Foreign Economic Policy, 1945-1950." Ph.D. Diss., University of North Carolina, 1983.

431 Salem, Ronald J. "East-West Trade Control Program." Ph.D. Diss., American University, 1958.

432 Spulber, Nicholas. "Effects of the Embargo on Soviet Trade." *Harvard Business Review* 30 (Nov./Dec. 1952), 122-128.

The 1972 Trade Agreements

The commercial agreements signed during the 1972 Moscow Summit garnered considerable interest. The U.S. Department of Commerce (entry 445) provides the basic documents, and the U.S. Senate Committee on Finance (entry 444) supplies additional background information. Contemporary commentaries focused on policy changes (Walter Krause and John Mathis, entry 438), legal aspects (Robert Starr, entry 441), trade prospects (John Huhs, entry 437), ramifications for the Soviet Union (Josef Brada and Arthur King, entry 434), and the advantages or disadvantages for the U.S. (Marshall Goldman, entry 435). As outlined in the text, the trade agreements failed when the U.S.S.R. balked at accepting congressionally mandated emigration quotas; see Nancy Stetson (entry 442).

433 Berman, Harold J. "The US-USSR Trade Agreement from a Soviet Perspective." *American Journal of International Law* 67 (July 1973), 516-522.

434 Brada, Josef C., and Arthur E. King. "The Soviet-American Trade Agreements: Prospects for the Soviet Economy." *Russian Review* 32 (Oct. 1973), 345-359.

435 Goldman, Marshall I. "Who Profits More from U.S.-Soviet Trade?" *Harvard Business Review* 51 (Nov./Dec. 1973), 79-87.

436 Grossman, Gregory. "Prospects and Policy for U.S.-Soviet Trade." *American Economic Review* 64 (May 1974), 289-293.

437 Huhs, John I. "Developing Trade with the Soviet Union." *The Columbia Journal of World Business* 8 (Fall 1973), 116-130.

438   Krause, Walter, and F. John Mathis. "The U.S. Policy Shift on East-West Trade." *Journal of International Affairs* 28 (1974), 25-37.

439   McMillan, Carl H., ed. *Changing Perspectives in East-West Commerce.* Lexington, MA: Lexington Books, 1974.

440   Parsons, A. Peter. "Recent Developments in East-West Trade: The U.S. Perspective." *Law and Contemporary Problems* 32 (Summer-Autumn 1972), 548-556.

441   Starr, Robert. "A New Legal Framework for Trade Between the United States and the Soviet Union: The 1972 US-USSR Trade Agreement." *American Journal of International Law* 67 (Jan. 1973), 63-83.

442   Stetson, Nancy Howard. "Congress and Foreign Policy: The 1972 U.S.-U.S.S.R. Trade Agreement and the Trade Reform Act." Ph.D. Diss., Columbia University, 1979.

443   Timberlake, Charles E., ed. *Detente: A Documentary Record.* New York: Praeger, 1978.

444   U.S. Congress, Senate Committee on Finance. *Background Materials Relating to the United States-Soviet Union Commercial Agreements.* Washington, DC: G.P.O., 1974.

445   U.S. Department of Commerce. *U.S.-Soviet Commercial Agreements 1972: Texts, Summaries and Supporting Papers.* Washington, DC: G.P.O., 1973.

U.S. Business Interest in Soviet Trade

At the close of World War II, Alexander Gerschenkron (entry 449), a distinguished economic historian, believed that the Soviets might move away from autarky and seek collaboration with the West. The Cold War quickly overshadowed this brief interlude of optimism. James Giffen (entry 450) prepared a legal guide to Soviet trade at the end of the 1960s when the U.S. government adopted a more benign attitude toward East-West commerce. Samuel Pisar (entry 458) wrote a similar text, which received plaudits from both business and academic communities. The leap in trade in the early 1970s prompted a spate of books; of special interest are Thomas Greer (entry 452) and the text by a team of experts in export management, Christopher Stowell, et al (entry 461). In the last half of the 1980s, Soviet reforms revived this

genre of literature; see Misha Knight (entry 454) and Boris
Bubnov (entry 446).

446 Bubnov, Boris. *Foreign Trade with the USSR: A Manager's
Guide to Recent Reforms.* New York: Pergamon, 1987.

447 De Pauw, John Whylen. *Soviet-American Trade Negotiations.*
New York: Praeger, 1979.

448 *Doing Business with the Russians.* New York: Praeger, 1979.

449 Gerschenkron, Alexander. *Economic Relations with the USSR.*
New York: Committee on International Economic Policy, 1945.

450 Giffen, James Henry. *The Legal and Practical Aspects of Trade
with the Soviet Union.* New York: Praeger, 1969.

451 Goldman, Marshall I. *Detente and Dollars: Doing Business with
the Soviets.* New York: Basic Books, 1975.

452 Greer, Thomas. *Marketing in the Soviet Union.* New York:
Praeger, 1973.

453 Heyman, Hans. *We Can Do Business With Russia.* New York:
Ziff-Davis, 1945.

454 Knight, Misha G. *How to do Business with Russians: A
Handbook and Guide for Western World Business People.* New
York: Quorum Books, 1987.

455 Marer, Paul, ed. *Eximbank and East-West Trade.* Bloomington:
Indiana University Press, 1975.

456 Margold, Stella K. *Let's Do Business with Russia.* New York:
Harper, 1948.

457 *A New Trade Policy toward Communist Countries.* New York:
Committee for Economic Development, 1972.

458 Pisar, Samuel. *Coexistence and Commerce: Guidelines for
Transactions Between East and West.* New York: McGraw-Hill,
1970.

459 Starr, Robert, ed. *Business Transaction with the USSR.* New
York: American Bar Association, 1975.

460 Starr, Robert. *East-West Business Transactions.* New York:
Praeger, 1974.

461 Stowell, Christopher E., et al. *Soviet Industrial Import Priorities:
With Marketing Considerations for Exporting to the USSR.* New
York: Praeger, 1975.

462 U.S. Congress, Senate Committee on Foreign Relations. *U.S.
Trade and Investments in the Soviet Union and Eastern Europe:*

The Role of Multinational Corporations. Washington, DC: G.P.O., 1974.

American Politics and Soviet Trade

After the strident period of the Cold War (see the first two subsections above), the U.S. political background to Soviet trade became both more flexible and complex. The Kennedy and Johnson administrations considered diplomacy and trade as twin tactics in the effort to influence or undermine Soviet power—see Paul Kubricht (entry 471) and *Report to the President of the Special Committee on U.S. Trade Relations* (entry 478). Gary Bertsch (entry 465) examines the political dimensions in U.S. trade with the U.S.S.R. from Nixon to Reagan and outlines the contradictory economic policies of the Carter administration. The European perspective on the interplay between U.S. politics and Soviet trade can be found in Jacobsen (entry 469) and Reinhard Rode (entry 479). James Millar (entry 474) demonstrates that the mixture of politics and commerce has had a negative impact on the U.S. economy. John Raley (entry 477) examines the U.S. economic response to the Afghanistan invasion and concludes that the sanctions hurt the U.S. more than Russia. For a government view of the same event, see Jack Brougher (entry 466).

463   An, Taeg Won. "Soviet Perceptions of Soviet-American Trade." Ph.D. Diss., University of Georgia, 1984.

464   Berman, Harold J. "A Reappraisal of U.S.-U.S.S.R. Trade Policy." *Harvard Business Review* 42 (July/Aug. 1964), 139-151.

465   Bertsch, Gary K. "American Politics and Trade with the USSR." In Bruce Parrott, ed. *Trade, Technology, and Soviet-American Relations*. Bloomington: Indiana University Press, 1985, pp. 243-282.

466   Brougher, Jack. "U.S.-U.S.S.R. Trade after Afghanistan." *Business America* 3 (7 Apr. 1980), 3-12.

467   Chapman, Margaret and Carl Marcy, eds. *Common Sense in U.S.-Soviet Trade*. Washington, DC: American Committee on East-West Accord, 1983.

468 Grub, Phillip D., and Karel Holbik. *American-East European Trade: Controversy, Progress, Prospects*. Washington, DC: National Press, 1969.

469 Jacobsen, Hanns-D. "U.S. Export Control and Export Administration Legislation." In Reinhard Rode and Hanns-D. Jacobsen, ed. *Economic Warfare or Detente: An Assessment of East-West Relations in the 1980s*. Boulder, CO: Westview, 1985, pp. 213-225.

470 Jamgotch, Nish, ed. *Sectors of Mutual Benefit in U.S.-Soviet Relations*. Durham, NC: Duke University Press, 1985.

471 Kubricht, A. Paul. "Politics and Foreign Policy: A Brief Look at the Kennedy Administration's Eastern European Diplomacy." *Diplomatic History* 11 (Winter 1987), 55-65.

472 Lavelle, Michael Joseph. "Soviet Image of the U.S. Economy, 1953-1963." Ph.D. Diss., Boston College, 1966.

473 Metzger, Stanley D. "Federal Regulation and Prohibition of Trade with Iron Curtain Countries." *Law and Contemporary Problems* 29 (1964), 1000-1018.

474 Millar, James R. "The Impact of Trade and Trade Denial on the U.S. Economy." In Bruce Parrott, ed. *Trade, Technology, and Soviet-American Relations*. Bloomington: Indiana University Press, 1985, pp. 324-350.

475 Miller, Mark Emory. "The Interplay of Politics and Economics in the U.S.-U.S.S.R. Relationship: 1969-1976." Ph.D. Diss., University of Miami, 1978.

476 Pubantz, Jerry. "Marxism-Leninism and Soviet-American Economic Relations Since Stalin." *Law and Contemporary Problems* 37 (Summer-Autumn 1972), 535-547.

477 Raley, John Gordon. "The Use of Economic Sanctions as a Political Weapon in U.S.-Soviet Relations." Ph.D. Diss., University of Massachusetts, 1986.

478 *Report to the President of the Special Committee on U.S. Trade Relations*. Washington, DC: G.P.O., 1965.

479 Rode, Reinhard. "The United States." In Reinhard Rode and Hanns-D. Jacobsen, ed. *Economic Warfare or Detente: An Assessment of East-West Relations in the 1980s*. Boulder, CO: Westview, 1985, pp. 184-199.

480 Tender, Lisa Maria. "The Foreign Policy Aspects of U.S.-Soviet Trade Relations in the Early 1970s." Ph.D. Diss., Tufts University, 1980.

481   U.S. Congress, Joint Economic Committee. *East-West Commercial Policy: A Congressional Dialogue with the Reagan Administration.* Washington, DC: G.P.O., 1982.

482   U.S. Congress, Senate Committee on Banking, Housing, and Urban Affairs. *U.S. Embargo of Food and Technology to the Soviet Union.* Washington, DC: G.P.O., 1980.

483   U.S. Senate. *Reauthorization of the Export Administration Act.* Washington, DC: G.P.O., 1983.

484   U.S. State Department. *American Foreign Policy: Basic Documents 1977-1980.* Washington, DC: G.P.O., 1983.

485   Wright, Robert B. "American Economic Diplomacy and the Soviet Bloc." *Social Science* 34 (Oct. 1959), 200-217.

The Grain Trade

Nick Butler (entry 487) and James Jones (entry 489) place the grain trade in its international context. There are voices of concern over this trade (James Trager, entry 491), but a strong American consensus supports such commerce; see Bertsch (entry 465) and Rode (entry 479). Franklin Vargo (entry 495) explains the rationale for the expansion of agriculturally-related U.S. exports to the U.S.S.R. during Reagan's second term of office. The significance of this trade for American agribusiness is revealed by the amount of periodical literature issued on this topic by the U.S. Department of Agriculture (entries 492 and 493 as samples). See also the works listed above in the agriculture subsection of The Soviet Economy and Foreign Trade.

486   Biggs, Tyler Sanford. "Political Economy of East-West Trade: The Case of the 1972-1973 U.S.-Russian Wheat Deal." Ph.D. Diss., University of California, 1976.

487   Butler, Nick. *The International Grain Trade: Problems and Prospects.* New York: St. Martin's, 1986.

488   Gavin, Joseph Gleason. "The Political Economy of U.S. Agricultural Export Policy, 1971-1975: Government Response to a Changing Economic Environment." Ph.D. Diss., Columbia University, 1980.

489   Jones, James R., ed. *East-West Agricultural Trade.* Boulder, CO: Westview, 1986.

490 Qasmi, Bashir Aslam. "An Analysis of the 1980 U.S. Trade Embargo on Exports of Soybeans and Soybean Products to the Soviet Union: A Spatial Price Equilibrium Approach." Ph.D. Diss., Iowa State University, 1986.

491 Trager, James. *The Great Grain Robbery*. New York: Ballantine, 1975.

492 U.S. Agriculture Department. *USSR Grain Situation and Outlook* (9 Feb. 1988), 1-8.

493 U.S. Agriculture Department. "U.S./Soviet Grain." *FAS Fact Sheet* (22 May 1987), 1-4.

494 U.S. Congress, Senate Committee on Agriculture, Nutrition, and Forestry. *Embargo on Grain Sales to the Soviet Union*. Washington, DC: G.P.O., 1980.

495 Vargo, Franklin J. "U.S.-U.S.S.R. Trade Climate Improves, But Soviet Import Ability Weakens." *Business America* 9 (21 July 1986), 6-8.

The U.S., Soviets, and the Western Alliance

The U.S. cannot implement in isolation an economic policy toward the Soviet Union. Jozef Wilczynski (entry 507) concludes that since 1945 commerce has been increasingly conditioned by economic self-interest. Angela Stent (entry 504) examines the Soviet trade of the U.S., West Germany, France, United Kingdom, and Japan, using the pipeline controversies from 1962 to illustrate contrasting perspectives. Stephen Woolcock (entry 508) examines the clash between American and European trade policy over the Polish crisis, while Stent (entry 505) presents the case for a strategic trade policy. Experts (Abraham Becker, entry 496) note that the U.S. is not likely to obtain allied agreement on a trade policy that restricts commercial relations with the East. See Gary Bertsch (entry 497) for a focused study of CoCom.

496 Becker, Abraham S., ed. *Economic Relations with the USSR: Issues for the Western Alliance*. Lexington, MA: Lexington Books, 1983.

497 Bertsch, Gary K. *East-West Strategic Trade, COCOM and the Atlantic Alliance*. Paris: Atlantic Institute, 1983.

498   Ellison, Herbert J., ed. *Soviet Policy toward Western Europe: Implications for the Atlantic Alliance.* Seattle: University of Washington Press, 1983.

499   Fallenbuchl, Zbigniew M., and Carl H. McMillan, eds. *Partners in East-West Economic Relations: The Determinants of Choice.* New York: Pergamon, 1980.

500   Hamilton, Daniel Sheldon. "The Carrot and the Stick: German and American Approaches to East-West Trade, 1945-1985." Ph.D. Diss., Johns Hopkins University, 1985.

501   Harvey, Mose L. *East-West Trade and United States Policy.* New York: National Association of Manufacturers, 1966.

502   Lowenfeld, David. "The Alliance Politics of East-West Trade." Ph.D. Diss., Harvard University, 1987.

503   Smith, Gordon B., ed. *The Politics of East-West Trade.* Boulder, CO: Westview Press, 1984.

504   Stent, Angela E. "East-West Economic Relations and the Western Alliance." In Bruce Parrott, ed. *Trade, Technology, and Soviet-American Relations.* Bloomington, Indiana University Press, 1985, pp. 283-323.

505   Stent, Angela E., ed. *Economic Relations with the Soviet Union: American and West German Perspectives.* Boulder, CO: Westview, 1985.

506   Ullman, Richard H., and Mario Zucconi, eds. *Western Europe and the Crisis in U.S.-Soviet Relations.* New York: Praeger, 1987.

507   Wilczynski, Jozef. *The Economics and Politics of East-West Trade.* New York: Praeger, 1969.

508   Woolcock, Stephen. "East-West Trade: U.S. Policy Versus European Interests." *Soviet and East European Foreign Trade* 19 (Spring 1983), 3-16.

Technology Transfer

Josef Brada (entry 512) presents an old but still useful overview of the transfer of technology and discusses the arguments supporting and opposing stringent controls. Jurgen Notzold (entry 520) notes that foreign trade has accounted for only a small percent of Soviet GNP, that much of this trade has been with Comecon, and that food has absorbed a major portion of Soviet imports from the West. While Antony Sutton (entry 524) makes excessive claims for the influence of Western technology on the U.S.S.R., Philip Hanson (entry 515) argues that the impact has been less than one-half of one percent of the annual growth of the Soviet Union's net industrial product. Jan Monkiewicz and Jan Maciejewicz (entry 519) break relatively new ground in their examination of reverse (East to West) technology transfer.

509 Ailes, Catherine P., and Arthur E. Pardee, Jr. *Cooperation in Science and Technology: An Evaluation of the U.S.-Soviet Agreement.* Boulder, CO: Westview, 1986.

510 Bertsch, Gary K., and John R. McIntyre, eds. *National Security and Technology Transfer: The Strategic Dimensions of East-West Trade.* Boulder, CO: Westview, 1983.

511 Brada, Josef C. "Soviet-Western Trade and Technology Transfer: An Economic Overview." In Bruce Parrott, ed. *Trade, Technology, and Soviet-American Relations.* Bloomington, Indiana University Press, 1985.

512 Brada, Josef C. *Technology Transfer between the United States and the Countries of the Soviet Bloc.* Trieste: Istituto di Studi e Documentazione sull'Est Europeo, 1981.

513 Central Intelligence Agency. *USSR: Role of Foreign Technology in the Development of the Motor Vehicle Industry.* Washington, DC: G.P.O., 1979.

514 Crawford, Beverly Kay. "Beyond Profit and Power: State Intervention and International Collaboration in East-West Technology Transfer." Ph.D. Diss., University of California, 1982.

515 Hanson, Philip. *Trade and Technology in Soviet-Western Relations.* New York: Columbia University Press, 1981.

516 Holliday, George D. *Technology Transfer to the USSR, 1928-1937 and 1966-1975: The Role of Western Technology in Soviet Economic Development.* Boulder, CO: Westview, 1979.

517 Larrabee, F. Stephen. *Technology and Change in East-West Relations.* Boulder, CO: Westview, 1988.

518 Liefert, William Mark. "The Economic Gain to the USSR from Trade with the OECD in 1972 and 1976." Ph.D. Diss., University of Michigan, 1986.

519 Monkiewicz, Jan, and Jan Maciejewicz. *Technology Export from the Socialist Countries.* Boulder, CO: Westview, 1986.

520 Notzold, Jurgen. "Technology Transfer." In Reinhard Rode and Hanns-D. Jacobsen, eds. *Economic Warfare or Detente: An*

Assessment of East-West Relations in the 1980s. Boulder, CO: Westview, 1985, pp. 50-62.

521   Schroeder, Wayne Alan. "Soviet-American Technology Transfer and United States National Security." Ph.D. Diss., University of Southern California, 1981.

522   *Scientific Communication and National Security.* 2 vols. Washington, DC: National Academy of Sciences, 1982.

523   Seward, Bernard L., Jr., ed. *Technology Control, Competition, and National Security: Conflict and Consensus.* Lanham, MD: University Press of America, 1987.

524   Sutton, Antony C. *Western Technology and Soviet Economic Development, 1945 to 1965.* Stanford, CA: Hoover Institution Press, 1973.

525   Wasowski, Stanislaw, ed. *East-West Trade and the Technology Gap: A Political and Economic Appraisal.* New York: Praeger, 1970.

526   Zalenski, Eugene, and Helgard Wienert. *Technology Transfer between East and West.* Paris: Organization for Economic Cooperation and Development, 1980.

BIBLIOGRAPHIES

There are no bibliographies devoted exclusively to American-Russian/Soviet economic relations; nevertheless, basic English-language sources can be found in Richard Burns (entry 531). For works published since 1982, consult the book review sections of journals devoted to business, economics, history, and international relations. The best annotated bibliography of Western-language sources on Russia and the Soviet Union is by Paul Horecky (entry 542), supplemented by Stephan Horak (entry 540) as well as the annual *American Bibliography of Russian and East European Studies* (entry 527). Sometimes the only scholarly studies on certain aspects of economic relations can be found in dissertations, see Jesse Dossick (entries 533 & 534), updated annually in the Winter issue of *Slavic Review.* Since 1979, *Diplomatic History* has supplied dissertation titles on U.S. foreign relations in each Spring issue. Agencies of the U.S. government have prepared various guides (entries 529, 538,

547, 551), and for current government materials see the *Monthly Catalog of United States Government Publications* (entry 550). The best source for periodical literature is *Interflo: An East-West Trade News Monitor*, which lists and summarizes 400 to 500 newspaper and magazine articles each month.

527 *The American Bibliography of Russian and East European Studies.* Bloomington: Indiana University Press, 1957-.

528 American Historical Association. *Guide to Historical Literature.* New York: Macmillan, 1961-.

529 Basler, Roy P., et al., eds. *A Guide to the Study of the United States of America.* Washington, DC: Library of Congress, 1960.

530 Bolkhovitinov, N. N. *Russia and the United States: A Survey of Soviet Archival Documents and Historical Research.* Armonk, NY: M. E. Sharpe, 1987.

531 Burns, Richard Dean. *Guide to American Foreign Relations since 1700.* Santa Barbara, CA: ABC-Clio, 1983.

532 Dexter, Byron, with Elizabeth H. Bryant and Janice L. Murray, eds. *The Foreign Affairs Fifty-Year Bibliography: New Evaluation of Significant Books on International Relations, 1920-1970.* New York: Bowker, 1972.

533 Dossick, Jesse J. *Doctoral Research on Russia and the Soviet Union.* New York: New York University Press, 1960.

534 Dossick, Jesse J. *Doctoral Research on Russia and the Soviet Union, 1960-1975.* New York: Garland, 1976.

535 *Foreign Affairs Bibliography: A Selected and Annotated List of Books on International Relations.* New York: Harper, 1933-.

536 Friedel, Frank, ed. *Harvard Guide to American History.* 2 vols. Cambridge, CA: Harvard University Press, 1974.

537 Hammond, Thomas T., comp. and ed. *Soviet Foreign Relations and World Communism: A Selected, Annotated Bibliography of 7,000 Books in Thirty Languages.* Princeton, NJ: Princeton University Press, 1965.

538 Heleniak, Timothy E. *Bibliography of Soviet Statistical Handbooks.* Washington, DC: U.S. Bureau of the Census, 1988.

539 Hernes, Helga. *The Multinational Corporation: A Guide to Information Sources.* Detroit, MI: Gale, 1977.

540 Horak, Stephan M., ed. *Russia, the USSR and Eastern Europe: A Bibliographical Guide to English Language Publications, 1964-1974*. Littleton, CO: Libraries Unlimited, 1978.

541 Horecky, Paul L., ed. *Basic Russian Publications: A Selected and Annotated Bibliography on Russia and the Soviet Union.* Chicago: University of Chicago Press, 1962.

542 Horecky, Paul L. *Russia and the Soviet Union: A Bibliographic Guide to Western-Language Publications.* Chicago: University of Chicago Press, 1965.

543 Jones, David L. *Books in English on the Soviet Union, 1917-73: A Bibliography.* New York: Garland, 1975.

544 Kanet, Roger E. *Soviet and East European Foreign Policy: A Bibliography of English-and Russian-Language Publica-tions, 1967-1971.* Santa Barbara, CA: ABC-Clio, 1974.

545 LaBarr, Dorothy F., and J. David Singer. *The Study of International Politics: A Guide to the Sources for the Student, Teacher, and Researcher.* Santa Barbara, CA: ABC-Clio, 1976.

546 Morley, Charles. *Guide to Research in Russian History.* Syracuse: Syracuse University Press, 1951.

547 Orr, Oliver H., Jr. *Guide to the Study of the United States of America: Supplement 1956-1965.* Washington, DC: Library of Congress, 1976.

548 Pfaltzgraff, Robert L., Jr. *The Study of International Relations: A Guide to Information Sources.* Detroit. MI: Gale, 1977.

549 Shapiro, David. *A Select Bibliography of Works in English on Russian History, 1801-1917.* Oxford: Basil Blackwell, 1962.

550 U.S. Superintendent of Documents. *Monthly Catalog of United States Government Publications.* Washington, DC: G.P.O., 1895-.

551 *U.S.-U.S.S.R. Trade: Selected List of Sources.* Washington, DC: U.S. Department of Commerce, Jan. 1981.

552 Wheeler, Lora Jeanne. *International Business and Foreign Trade: Information Sources.* Detroit, MI: Gale, 1968.

553 Zawodny, J. K. *Guide to the Study of International Relations.* San Francisco, CA: Chandler, 1966.

AUTHOR INDEX

SUBJECT INDEX